A METAPOETICS OF THE PASSAGE

OVERLEAF:

Passage de l'Opéra, leading to Boulevard des Italiens, end of nineteenth century; Bibliothèque de la ville de Paris, *photo courtesy of Roger Viollet.*

À L'ENTRESOL
HENRI CELLARIUS NEVEU
COURS DE DANSE
CELLARIUS
SALON EXPOSITION

A METAPOETICS OF THE PASSAGE

Architextures in Surrealism and After

MARY ANN CAWS

UNIVERSITY PRESS OF NEW ENGLAND
HANOVER AND LONDON
1981

UNIVERSITY PRESS OF NEW ENGLAND
Brandeis University
Brown University
Clark University
Dartmouth College
University of New Hampshire
University of Rhode Island
Tufts University
University of Vermont

Library of Congress Catalogue Card Number 80-54468
International Standard Book Number 0-87451-194-1

Printed in the United States of America

Library of Congress Cataloging in Publication data
will be found on the last printed page of this book.

Publication of this volume has been aided by a grant from the
NATIONAL ENDOWMENT FOR THE HUMANITIES.

for
HENRI PEYRE

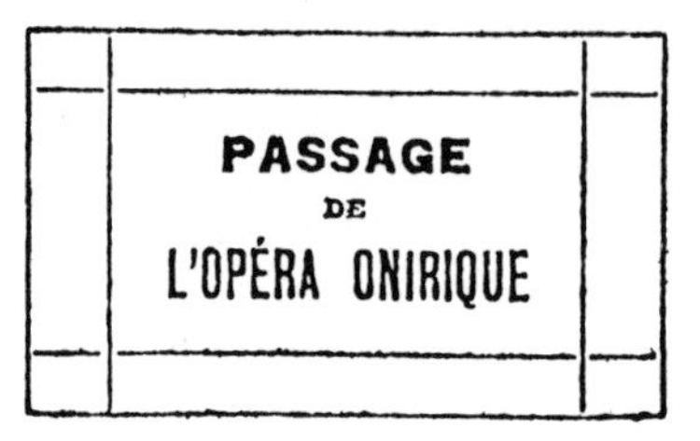

Je ne puis asseurer mon objet; il va trouble
et chancelant, d'une yvresse naturelle. Je le
prens en ce poinct, comme il est, en l'instant
que je m'amuse à luy: je ne peinds pas l'estre,
je peinds le passage*; non un passage d'aage en*
autre, ou, comme dict le peuple, de sept en
sept ans, mais de jour en jour, de minute en minute.
Il faut accomoder mon histoire à l'heure. . . .

Une femme passa. . .
Ailleurs, bien loin d'ici! Jamais *peut-etre!*
Car j'ignore où tu fuis, tu ne sais où je vais,
O toi que j'eusse aimée, ô toi qui le savais!

Passeur passe jusqu'au trépas
. . .
Il faut passer il faut passer
Passer et puis recommencer

. . . à la limite des deux jours qui opposent
la réalité extérieure au subjectivisme du passage,
comme un homme qui se tient au bord de ses abîmes,
sollicité également par les courants d'objets
et par les tourbillons de soi-même, dans cette
zone étrange où tout est lapsus, lapsus de l'attention
et de l'inattention, arrêtons-nous un peu pour
éprouver ce vertige.

I cannot fix my object with any sureness; it goes
along disturbed and wavering, with a natural tipsiness.
I take it in this moment, as it is, in the instant I am
interested in: *I do not paint being, I paint passage*;
not a passage from one age to another, or as they say,
from one seven-year span to the next, but from day to
day, from minute to minute. I must make my story match
the time. . .

MICHEL EYQUEM DE MONTAIGNE, *Essais*

A woman passed by. . .
Elsewhere, so far from here! Perhaps *never!*
For I know not where you flee, you know not where I go.
Oh how I would have loved you, oh how you knew!

CHARLES BAUDELAIRE, "A une passante"

Passer pass on until the passing

. . .

Pass one must pass one must
Pass and then start over

GUILLAUME APOLLINAIRE, "Les Bacs"

. . . at the limit of the two daylights which oppose
exterior reality to the subjectivism of the passage,
like a man holding back at the edge of his abysses,
equally attracted by the currents of objects and by the
tornadoes of himself, in this strange zone where everything is distraction of attention and of inattention,
let us halt a moment to experience this vertigo.

LOUIS ARAGON, *Le Paysan de Paris*

CONTENTS

ACKNOWLEDGMENTS

The preparation of this manuscript was originally made possible by the John Simon Guggenheim Memorial Foundation, by a Senior Fulbright-Hays travel grant, and by the Research Foundation of the City University of New York.

The text has been developed over a lengthy period; some material has previously appeared in print and is now greatly revised. My thanks to the editors and presses concerned for permission to use and in some cases to recast the following: "Making the Crossing: Valéry's Sea into Hart Crane's Scene," in *Analysis of Literary Texts: Current Trends in Methodology*, vol. 3 (New York: Bilingual Press, York College of CUNY, 1979); "A Poetics of the Surrealist Passage," in *Twentieth Century Literature*, Surrealism Issue 21, 1 (Feb. 1979); and first versions of the Deguy and Garelli essays in *Sub-Stance* 5/6 (1973), and 10 (1976), as well as of the Dupin essay in *Dalhousie French Studies* 1 (1979); the chapter on René Char was originally published in *World Literature Today*, Char Issue (Summer 1977).

Grateful acknowledgment is made to the publishers of the following works, containing the poems quoted: Louis Aragon (*Feu de joie* © Gallimard, 1920); André Breton (*Poèmes* © Gallimard, 1948); René Char (*Chants de la Balandrane* © Gallimard, 1978); Hart Crane (*The Complete Poems and Selected Letters and Prose* © Doubleday, 1966); Robert Desnos (*Domaine public* © Gallimard, 1943); Michel Deguy (*Poèmes de la presqu'île* © Gallimard, 1961, *Biefs* © Gallimard, 1964, *Poèmes* © Gallimard, 1972); Jacques Dupin (*L'Embrasure* © Gallimard, 1972, *Dehors* © Gallimard, 1975); Paul Eluard (*Capitale de la douleur* © Gallimard, 1926); James Merrill (*Nights and Days* © Atheneum, 1966); Octavio Paz (*Early Poems 1935–1955* © Indiana University Press, 1973); Paul Valéry (*Poèmes* © Gallimard, 1942).

To my students at Hunter College, at the Graduate Center of the

City University of New York (in particular, in Comparative Poetics: Sylvia Goldfrank, Deborah Sinnreich, Walton Van Winkle, and Patricia Zaccardo), and at Princeton University, my gratitude for having accompanied my explorations into many of these passages, to Hilary Caws, for indexing them, and to Peter Caws, my even warmer gratitude for making them less murky.

PREFACE

The essays in this volume, with their connections and interconnections, are situated around the enabling metaphor of passage, taken in its several senses. The initial section discusses the interrelations of act and image: breach or rupture, the steps of passage and the phenomenon of traversal, as illustrated first by a crossing of one text remembered into another, within the reader's mind and under the explicit title of a poem called "Passage." The central body of material in the second and third sections relates to surrealism, whose chosen images of communicating vessels and swinging doors facilitate metamorphosis, as its fluid atmosphere facilitates exchange. The last section concerns the theoretical and textual ventures of four contemporary poets, under the heading of a metapoetic consciousness as the end result of the temporal passage between the surrealists and our epoch. Surrealism itself is taken as the major corridor of exchange, so that its passage and its passages lend their shape to the present text.

The readings included represent what I have called a "surrealist baroque" (in which I include Scève, Góngora, and Desnos), surrealism itself (Breton, Aragon, Eluard, and Desnos), as well as the contemporary poetry marked by it (Paz, Merrill), and, on the French side of things, Char, Garelli, Deguy, and Dupin. The metaphor of passage initiating the discussion is not meant to be binding in its control, but only to be a metaphor of the metaphor of linking, which may illuminate some poetic and metapoetic corridors without weighing hard upon them.

Surrealism is an ideal starting place for a meditation upon passage. Its basic philosophy opens it to flux and all its metaphors condemn such narrowing limits as "literary" reason might dictate, and such typing by category as might be acceptable in other approaches; surrealism's "sublime point" is convergence actualized, the meeting place of opposite categories, whereas one of its privileged games and several of its privileged images are based upon the notions of flux and crossings-over, of substances and sentiments and perceptions merging into others, of the imaginary mixing with the real. The lessons of passage this movement propounds should occasion flux and flexibility of response within the reading itself, as the reading eye is presumed to refuse separation between itself and the object perceived, as in the combinatory and fusing realm of surrealist vision. The works of the poets referred to in these pages: Breton, Desnos, Aragon, Paz, Eluard, and Merrill,[1] participate in the attitudes and images of openness, even self-consciously, in the interchange between elements and the moments of shift and turn. They exemplify a threshold awareness[2] as the entrance to a new kind of "architextural" dwelling.

The use of the term "architexture" is meant quite simply to call attention to the surface texture of the construction made by reading. As architecture involves etymologically both the concept of origin and that of the building process, architexture would involve both construction and material texture, would concentrate upon their interplay. As architecture situates the building in its world, so architexture situates the text in the world of other texts.[3]

The architexture of a particular work refers to the structure of the connecting passage, bridge, or corridor between elements as it relates to the material of the text or to that stretching between two texts, as in the example of Crane and Valéry. Furthermore, a complex interior metapoetic or metatextual structure is built up in the reader's mind, as many contemporary critics point out, on the basis of a progressive acquaintance with a number of texts of the same sort. So this relation counts equally with the initial perception, as the structural counts equally with the instinctive reaction to the material feel of the text: thus the juxtapositional term of architexture, combining the two elements, and crossing their building parts.

The goal of an architextural reading is a constant awareness of surface tension and texture, easily dulled by exposure and by the easier grasp of message or plot or visible statement: texture includes visual and aural aspects of the text, available to a prolonged perception. The purpose of the present essays is to point and draw attention to the building that connects the individual text to a larger whole, as well as to the constructive material in its dimensionality as in its surface appearance, and to the reader's building on and in the passage[4] of the poem, in the fullest active and passive senses of that term.

This disquisition on a metaphor is also to be taken as an illustration of its own subject, for the approach to reading as performance and as passage, in particular relation to texts of exchange and cityscapes of passage, is already a self-reflective enterprise. That this should lead to the examination of some contemporary metapoetic passages of theory and practice is a further reflection on how the corridor makes and traces its own mobile construction, in which the reader participates. The very approach taken is meant to force a reading and re-reading of some familiar and less familiar passages as dwellings of the modern mind.

For all the quoted passages, the translations are mine, as are the decisions when to give the original and when not. In general, for poetry as well as for obviously poetic texts whose style requires the original as well as my translation—even if they are apparently in "prose"—two languages appear, whereas for prose that, again in my estimation, is more "straightforward" only the translation appears.

I. INTERRUPTION AND TRAVERSAL

THE BREACH OF THE POEM

J'entre donc par la brèche au cri rapide.
Thus I enter by the break with rapid cry.
YVES BONNEFOY, *Dans le leurre du seuil*

In recent literature and art, the techniques of the perishable have been cultivated with care by writers and artists, and received enthusiastically. Gaetan Picon comments on our reaction to the traces of older visual art and on its paradoxical appeal, in the present, from the past: "For we love the cracked surface, the traces of bygone coloring, the mutilation of the heads . . . for we love the death we ceaselessly live."[1] Applying his statement to the verbal arts, I would like to suggest that it is often in an obsession with the vanishing trace that contemporary poetry finds a sure source, that it is often a fascination with aborted action that lends to present meditations on poetic gesture their essential gravity.

The permanence of line as a criterion of value now so widely abandoned both in criticism and in creative work was based on a conception of the word and of the world more fixed than our present conception. The ramifications are multiple. For example, instead of taking, as it might have formerly, the inevitability of death as an invitation to a stylistic *carpe diem*, negativity underlining the brevity of our passage, rendered thereby artistically intense and aesthetically tragic, contemporary thought takes the assurance of eventual and also momentary cessation as the basic element of a vital rhythm whose significance is visible or audible only through its periodic differences or recurring interruptions. This principle is directly responsible for much of the poetic theory represented in these pages, particularly the concluding ones.

The word is situated, as Jacques Garelli reminds us, between two deaths, so that each cluster of sounds located within this regenerating rhythm is subsequently able to resume its impetus, thus refreshed, as if it were starting again. On the purely formal level, if the poem is a line of tension, then the interruption of that tension is responsible for the sudden but sure provision of new energy: "By its discontinuous rhythm, the poem inaugurates. . . ."[2] Given this context, the lesson of André Breton's paradoxical line, originally applied to love: "Always for the first time"[3] may be considered to be as significant in the matter of style as in that of sentiment. To be surrealistically valid, an act, whether linguistic, moral, or political, must throw off its past charge, adopting a position always primary. The accent falls on beginning, never on completion, on transformation rather than on stability. "Of course I only like," said Breton, "unfinished things." But—and we might ask the question for poetics and poetry in general—how is metamorphosis to be at once constant and freshly perceived, "always for the first time"?

THE NUL MOMENT REVALUED

Let me assume, for a moment, the fruitfulness of an obsession, however perverse, with the nullity or neutrality of a certain kind of instant in the text—with what Breton calls the *moment nul*.[4] Now the reaction of reader and author may be understandably, even profitably, different and may differ differently, depending on the time of reading. But I want to limit myself to one case, in the present moment. For example, the reader's occasional reaction to exactly the kind of pause Breton considered a nul moment—description, digression, identical repetition that he or she would ordinarily tend to bypass—may in fact repay more interest than the ordinary attention directed to those points the author seems to designate as the summits of the work. (I will not succumb here to the temptation of elaborating on the "seems," but will simply point it out.) This reader, engaged in a second reading of *Nadja*, may find—as I do—Breton's surprise that Nadja did not content herself with simply turning away her head when the flag passes, or his boredom with her lengthy reading of the menu, or his affirmation, on a certain day, that he could expect nothing interesting from her, more illuminating than the expected initial fascination with her madness. Breton's final turning away, that is, may have an impact on the reader more intense than his turning toward: thus, the nullity of interest on the author's part becomes the potential source of a renewed involvement for the reader. Furthermore, the two places in *Nadja* exerting the strongest appeal may well be, first, the series of three dots, "points de suspension" preceding the sentence "I had, some time ago, ceased to get along with Nadja,"[5] and then the gap typographically responding to that one, two pages later, between Breton's confession that he was perhaps unprepared for the proposal of genuine "amour fou," that irrational passion that she attached to him, and the exterior, objective sentence, which is to say, the literally alienating phrase: "They came, a few months ago, to tell me that Nadja was mad."[6] In short, the passages isolated, set apart by the author as evident high points, put in relief by a climax of lyricism, or obvious aphorising, by either extreme rapidity or extreme slowness of action, may not coincide with the high points of the reader's attention. The moment apparently perceived by the writer as nul—placed in ellipsis—may turn out to be, on some of the most valuable occasions, the reader's summit.

But of course the interval cherished, even in that contrary fashion, for its apparent (or real) dullness must not simply turn into an accentuation of oddity, paving the way for a too facile reversal like the romantic dogma of the hideous as beautiful; the stress placed by author or reader on moments of interruption between tense or meaningful action must be allowed its own extension even into dullness, without an instant conversion into its contrary.

INTERRUPTION

The tendency or temptation to completion (as in Gestalt theory, for instance) should not be used to divert the reading mind from the essential nature of the interruption considered as a privileged space. Francis Ponge sees the writing of a work as the stopping-up of a hole as do Leiris and Garelli: "boucher le trou," "supprimer le vide," "obturer le trou," "combler une fissure." Garelli continues: "So it is with poetry, fruit of nothingness projected blind into a verbal tumult secreting its images to fill in a fissure eating away like anguish, at an approximate world, always placed on the bias: the poem."[7] But poetry is not just the deliberate and positive reconquering of negative space. It can also be, at certain moments, the negation of any prosaic perception of wholeness, and the valuing of that negation as such. Thus René Daumal maintains that "all poetry has its root in the immediate act of negation"; René Char acknowledges, within the space of poetry, "the split produced by the appearance of being"; Leiris takes as his basis the "haut mal" or noble malady resulting from the crevices in the mind; and Yves Bonnefoy offers us a lyric statement of absence and dispersion as manifestations of the concretizing power of the poetic impulse: "Oh presence affirmed by the explosion of all its parts! To the extent it is present, the object never stops disappearing."[8]

Now in the examination, however brief, of the gap in the poem itself or the split within image and language, three separate aspects of self-conscious poetic rupture might be considered: first, the metaphors of division, which designate themselves as a commentary on poetry; second, the object at the center of the verbal labyrinth, seen as rent in two or exploded into many parts; and finally, the idea and the form of the broken apart as the clearest possible witnesses to meaningful creation.

The abundance of self-referential metaphors of rupture in the poetic vocabulary of the present is a sign of the distance separating the majority of contemporary theories and poems from the concluding perception of ideal continuity in such theories as the essential surrealist convergence of inside and outside, of object and sight, of center and link, exemplified by such poems as Breton's unforgettable "Vigilance": "Je ne touche plus que le coeur des choses/ je tiens le fil" ["I touch only the center of things/ I hold the thread"].[9] Whereas that latter perception is one of wholeness and necessary centrality, the best and most characteristic works of "recent" poetry are usually marked by fissure, fault, break, breach, gap, split, crevice, vacancy. The contrast is clear even in the titles: far removed from the overwhelming and touching optimism of such phrases as "L'Union Libre" ["Free Union"] or "L'Air de l'eau" ["The Air of Water"], where the accent falls on unity and conjunction, is the sharp contemporary consciousness of a rupture, often self-inflicted and usually unhesitatingly acknowledged: *Rupture, Coupure, L'Embrasure, Brèche, Failles, Fraction, Bifurs, Clivages, Partage formel, Paysages en deux*.

Furthermore, within the domain of the image itself, if the poem is still occasionally seen as a wall (a walled limit, bearing witness to solidity and coherence), that wall is most probably, as in the poems of Guillevic or Ponge, faulted in its desired continuity, its surface fissured inexorably and unreasonably, as Ponge puts it "Ces fautes . . . moins qu'à demi pardonnées." ["These faults . . . not even half-excused."][10] Within the already interrupted structure of the contemporary poetic frame, the most crucial images find themselves split apart, mirroring the exterior division. That is to say, the smallest element to which the poetic model can be reduced is itself fractured, as are all the larger frameworks into which the element is successively incorporated. Each collection of images focuses about a split or fissured center. If the poem is said to be a vessel, even a container of truth, then it will probably be presented as permanently cracked, so that this receptacle, whatever its form or importance, can never hold; while on the extreme and positive side of the metaphor, in such prose poems as Ponge's "La Cruche," the very word or material of poetry is said to be hollow. If, as in Yves Bonnefoy's *Pierre écrite*, the poem is presented as the contemporary analog of the traditional mystic or alchemical work, then the philosophical stone is no longer intact, but is rent asunder. The revivified Arthurian legend of the sword inserted in the rock reaffirms the high calling of poetry and the ultimate strength of poetic perception, intensifies the metaphors of its application, divisive and difficult to retract. The split stone is doubly rent by the ambivalence in its meaning, since the heroic gesture it summons is at once sadistic and noble.

If, in the unspoken pact between reader and poet, the poem is an implicit promise—of the synchronicity of its own time and space in the passages traversed and of its own space as sufficient—it is also now seen as the breach of that promise. Apollinaire taught us, long ago, the value of surprise in general; Bonnefoy teaches us the specific paradoxical carrying power of the poet's voice breaking, of the mute *e* as a "fault" deliberately chosen in French poetic form, of an "imperfection" seen as the summit of experience. The faulted form suits the poetic discourse riddled with those absences Bonnefoy calls the "signs consumed by the presence, close by, of the value they evoke."[11] The poem as pure *thereness* can best be experienced at the places where it reveals its pain; poetic language is replete with expressions of the moment "when the poem is rent apart":[12] thus the epigraph for this initial essay.

One school of contemporary theoreticians treats the text as if it were a syntagmatic succession of linguistic comments on a dispersed message; another implies an empty code, where the signifying moments are paradoxically nullified, or the referents eradicated at their core. The reader need only compare with Breton's vision of the unbroken chain of universal perception, where no link is missing, Michel Deguy's infinitely less lofty image of the rope of pearls around the neck of the poem to see how the holistic marvel of poetry as attitude appears to have suffered a diminishment, even a degradation, taken etymologically in its strict sense, that of descending steps.

RECUPERATION

However, it is just here that a reversal is evident, a recuperation of value oriented along the same lines as the metaphor of shipwreck at the turn of the century and shortly after. The wandering mind thinks not just of Stéphane Mallarmé, but of André Gide, Guillaume Apollinaire, and Robert Desnos—all of whom celebrate the stranded vessel of adventure precisely in its very immobilization, for that very immobilization becomes the source of myth from which a part of lyricism will derive its strength and around which subsequent ventures may focus.

Most contemporary definitions and analyses of the poem treat its own self-validating structure, whether or not they agree with Michael Riffaterre's assertion that there *is* no exterior referent to the poem.[13] In general, they manifest an intense consciousness of irregularity, of discontinuous pattern, of imperfection and flaw, with an evident delight in that consciousness. For Deguy, the poem is comparable to the quite humble arrangement of the whitewashed wall, the day, and the single leaf. For Bonnefoy, that single leaf is most valued as it is torn or dirtied, since that desired imperfection betrays its significance as an object marked by time and mortality. Here the reader might remember Wallace Stevens's "Poems of our Climate," refusing the perfection of a glass bowl of carnations in favor of the human imperfection of "Flawed words and stubborn sounds," the stuff, that is, of poetry. Jacques Dupin, once tempted—as we all were—by the notion of poetry dwelling in "high closed gardens," finally acknowledges it as the inescapable and painful "place where the opacity of the world seemed to open to the mingled stream of word, light and blood."[14] If indeed, the present poem is to be a serious undertaking, it is impossible ever to separate its project from the almost certain failure, and certain partiality, which the metaphors illustrate: painful birth, destruction, intense violence, both in substance and in form. This consciousness is finally productive, as a "fissure moving toward the work," as Garelli describes it.[15]

ENCLOSURE

Another avenue of investigation opens if we consider the distance subsisting within the poem as an enclosure, formally separate from the space of the nonpoem. Clearly, the poem itself is marked as an interval by the white exterior frame, that "murderous" margin standing in the same relation to the text as silence to the word; yet once taken into the poem, what might be called the "interior margin" serves as a fertile breach of the linear code, a fault acknowledged and profitable.

Finally, Jacques Derrida's description of *brisure* in its double sense of fault and articulation,[16] already in Littré's definition, and Michel Deguy's description of the notion of hinge, "a pleat, joint, interleaving, gap, breakage,"[17] might form the articulation for the turn from the idea of breach to that of passage. To complete this excursion around a metaphor, the edges of the text seen as enabling the experience of pleasure, according to Roland Barthes's description,[18] and the paradoxically inseparable parts of the cracked vessel of poetic language, the present replacement for the high-rigged vessels of symbolism and the communicating vessels of surrealism, point to the flaw as a source at last rediscovered for a renewal of the poem, seen in its passage and not in its perfected state. To change the metaphor, the cracked wall now replaces the swinging doors, those potentially marvelous *portes battantes* of the surrealist imagination, which open both on the dream and the real, but even in the wall's self-reference, it is effective as the embodiment of the poem's primary motion, a pulsation whose rhythm is slightly irregular as it translates the flaw in the construction or the breach in the code. Yet to this interruption in style and substance, which might have seemed negative, there corresponds a positive reawakening of poetic sensitivity in poet and reader, wherein what might have been construed as a negative breach in manners only, becomes a positive break, enabling the articulation of a *singular* manner.

FROM BREAK TO PASSAGE
Incursions and Excursions

> My job was to understand what these sudden fractures meant. I had the impression that I was keeping something open, an aperture pierced, in the verbal substance. And to such an extent that I then decided to make of that kind of understanding a method.
>
> YVES BONNEFOY, "La Fonction du poème"[1]

These essays take as their starting point the breach in the poem, that is, the realization that what was formerly construed as an whole—linguistic, literary, psychological—is most often seen at present as ruptured, its once continuous line or surface broken.[2] This interruption of poetic tradition makes way in its turn for a re-examination of the *incursion* of texts into other texts, and of their relations one to another in the corridor of the reader's mind, itself the place of passage.

The term "passage" may be taken as the corridor between moments, situations, states, at once spatial, temporal, psychological, sociological, and anthropological, its rites openly acknowledged. It is the place of ritual and psychological transformation, the moment of shift and displacement of sentiment, the consciousness of a textual turn. The notion of passage has also been extended to painting and sculpture, where it marks the instant of change, of colors blending one into the other, planes intersecting or of objects intersecting with the surrounding air, and so on. Originally associated with Paul Cézanne and the cubists, this sort of passage is a useful concept also for the critical eye.[3] Moreover, the idea may be likened to the *relais* in the weaving of a tapestry, that is, the moment at which there is a marked change of color or figure.[4] The varied techniques of joining patterns, covering over or disclosing passage or change, and the concept of rest between patterns—another shift, a relay as in a game, a relief between night and day—may also be useful in order to gain a different perspective on textual techniques. Connected with this guiding metaphor is the essential notion of the *step* (*pas*, Latin *passus*) both as in the steps of a stair (I have already hinted at this in the beginning pages, in relation to the term "degradation"), and also as in the steps of a walker or a passerby, in the "pasos" of Luis de Góngora, Breton's lost steps ("les pas perdus"),[5] and Louis Aragon's reference to the actual covered gallery *Passage de l'Opéra*,[6] all alluded to here. And in the steps taken between idea and idea in the mind of the reader, the two senses of the word may well join: in the following pages, that reader is eventually to be considered the *passenger*.

"I write," says Henri Michaux in his essay on passages, "in order to traverse myself."[7] For the poet, each ephemeral moment of perception or action is just as likely to be valued for its passing as for its substance: witness Baudelaire's "A une passante," already quoted, whose celebration of the brevity of the moment is in turn celebrated by Bonnefoy, for whom the reason of poetry itself is to name what passes. Of all the figures of traversal available to us, the most useful is Aragon's "Paris peasant," who strolls through the Passage de l'Opéra, an oneiric and yet real arcade, a gallery related etymologically to the opus or *oeuvre*. The poetics of the surrealist passage might well exemplify an attitude of *positive reversibility*, for author and reader. The equivocal nature of Aragon's evocations of this passage, illustrating the motto of "one-in-the-other," and related in nature to the guiding images of communicating vessels and swinging doors, means that it shall be given over neither to day nor to night, but to the world of the in-between, like the romantic *zweilicht* or between-two-lights. Compared by Aragon to a glassed-in ocean, both troubling and vertiginous, inspirational and obsessive in its effect, such an arcade allows and even forces perception to pass in both directions and all senses. The *passage* is by its nature devoted to the gesture of passing, and yet it may suffice as a dwelling place; exiguous, the space of the corridor is still the container for the expansive and extensive ambiguities of imagination at its most intense and for self-observation at its most lucid.

The Passage de l'Opéra also represents a dramatic opening and a stage corridor for theatrical entrances and exits, and these corridors may be transferred from their regular theatrical space to some *maison de passe* or brothel for the carnal and psychological satisfaction of the passerby. Its connecting ways furnish the behind-the-scenes and between-the-lines interest for the arcade, where the peasant of Paris walks, and where a text of meditation such as the following on the idea of passage might be inscribed:

> In this romantic boardinghouse given over to love, where the doors gape sometimes open like strange empty seashells, the arrangement of the premises exaggerates the already suspicious air lent it by the rather vulgar needs of a floating population. Long corridors like theater wings are strung with boxes, I mean rooms, all on the same side overlooking the passage, where a dual system of stairs provides two separate entries. Everything is contrived to facilitate hasty exits. (PP, 31)

The anticipated demolition of the Passage de l'Opéra, always devoted to the ephemeral, serves Aragon's purpose; surrealism is not a fact to be verified, but a state of mind to be celebrated, and the marvels of architecture survive only as text.

In the anthropological sense, the "passenger" undergoes a ritual ceremony of crossing or of liminality, becoming himself the site of "actions and reactions between the profane and the sacred" of which Arnold Van Gennep speaks in his work *The Rites of Passage*.[8] Van Gennep distinguishes successive stages in the human cycle: a time or space first of separation, "preliminary," in the preparatory instant to the liminary or marginal moment; in this stage the passenger is freed of ordinary costumes and daily ritual, opened to the extraordinary and the unaccustomed, cut off from before and after, and placed on the sill or *limen*, the psychological boundary of entrance and exit, always between two stages. Later, in the final or postliminary experience, at the stage of integration, the passenger will enter his new situation, changing his social and psychological status. But it is above all the middle, marginal, or liminary time that is of interest and has been continued in the work of succeeding theoreticians.

In his "Frame, Flow and Reflection: Ritual and Drama as Public Liminality,"[9] Victor Turner takes up once more after Van Gennep, and his own previous studies, the ceremonials of the *limen*, the patterns of the state of being-on-the-threshold, being-in-between, straddling two sides. In this "place that is not a place and this time that is not a time,"[10] a description that Turner applied to the liminal situation in his book entitled *Drama, Fields, and Metaphors*, the ritual passenger is a traveler without baggage and stripped of the usual signs, passing through various phases of role reversal, preparatory to assuming a new status. Liminal perception chooses its framework, hallowing an otherwise mundane space and setting it apart, as in a game whose rules oppose what happens therein to the normal customs of day-to-day work. Its time, in which the clock plays no role, remains extraordinary, and anything might happen in it. Comparing the liminal to the subjunctive mood in verbs, differentiated from the ordinary indicative mood of banal sociostructural activities, Turner emphasizes the potency of the liminal situation and its flexibility of application.

Recently Turner has applied the concept of liminal *stage* to the scene of any public performance, framing the section of experience to be set apart, whose costumes and masks mark the reversal of roles. The performance and its rules have, like the game, a ceremonial aspect, being sacralized and framed within the set, whose borders are clear and openly determined. To the ideas of threshold, passage, and framing, Turner adds the idea of flow, briefly summarized as an interior state in which action and perception are experienced conjointly, a state of awareness requiring neither goal nor reward outside of itself. (One of the chapters in my study will illustrate the idea of flow in textual perception.) The notion that the spectators reflect upon the action passionately leads Turner to cite Artaud's idea of theater as a violent expression of ritual liminality, removed, like alchemy, from the spectator, just as the world of magic is removed from the everyday, and framed within its own chosen limits.

Now may not the poem itself also and its reading be seen as passage, as a ceremonial made conscious in its preparation, its entrance, and its turns? The preceding theatrical reflection already illuminates the liminal and literary stage, implying the reader's own traversal of these rites of passage and locating in the text the threshold experience of *passing-through* and *crossing-over*: what more appropriate description of a poem than that it is self-identifying, self-sufficient, and self-determining (or posed as such by its author), that it chooses its frame and is held up to the observer for reflection? That the reflection is passionate for the observer or passerby may be a matter for debate; that the passerby or reader becomes the *passenger* in a proper reading is, I think, less so.

A chosen text can serve, then, as a ritual center of pilgrimage, liberating and regenerating the reader in its flux. (The rites of baptism, separation and incorporation, voyage through water or fire, gestures like the closing and opening of doors, the arranging of hair and masks, the scattering of herbs, and the actual crossing of the threshold: all the apparatus of the sacred or the profane may enter but are not essential.) The moment of the reader's own passage through the poem may be brief, and the potential charismatic power of the verbal manifestation may therefore go unperceived; but, like the automatic writing of the surrealists, the experience of such celebratory reading may outweigh the object or the result in importance. These essays, in their own flux, consider exemplary passages of several times and movements, treating these passages as separate spaces to be traversed one after the other in an *excursive* manner, or as the spaces of intermingling, of the crossing-over of two spaces into one another in the *incursive* manner; both excursions and incursions are enacted in and by the reader-as-passenger. The questions of interiority and exteriority or subjectivity and objectivity do not play a primary role on this stage of perception, in this passage of and through the text, where they too remain in flow.[11]

Finally, as for the relations between the passage perceived and the passage made, between passage as temporal and passage as spatial, I should like to conceive of them as remaining also in flow and flux, in an incursive state.

The two major uses in the text of the term "passage," as corridor and as a fixed place, are both in and for themselves architextural realities: connected by the metatextual idea of passage, and including the contrary notions of static and active, reflecting like mirrors placed across from each other, or like the image of the communicating vessels that are first used for the transport of the textual traveler toward the preferred *pages* and *passages* and *paysages* of surrealism. Figures, moments, scenes, elements, and words pass easily into one another, as do the viewer and the object viewed, perceiver and perceived: This is the justification, if one is needed, of the emphasis here not on explication and extensive references, but on textual implication. The scope of this readerly "errance" or wandering is meant to be at once limited and vast, using the metaphoric potentiality of passage as the hinge for some modest and investigative incursions and crossings among well-known texts, and then some theoretical and practical excursions among more recent poets. It is clear that the "errance," the incursion perceived or made, the excursion chosen, are all located, finally, in the working of the reader's mind in its response to the texts. The mapping in its interiority is at once determined and free, objectively guided and subjectively impassioned.

INTRODUCTORY PASSAGE
Valéry to Crane by the Sea

And so it was I entered the broken world.
HART CRANE, "The Broken Tower"

Among all the passages on passage, spatial, temporal, and literary, none is odder than Hart Crane's singular poem called "Passage."[1] Marianne Moore, rejecting it for *The Dial*, called it a poem without simplicity or "controlling force," and contemporary critics often consider it a failed voyage in search of, and never finding, even "an appropriate state of mind," whereas Crane himself thought it the "most interesting and conjectural thing" he wrote.[2]

I will give it two readings: the first, plain; the second, as the poem is parted by the prow of another poem, within the working and play of the reader's mind.

Where the cedar leaf divides the sky
I heard the sea.
In sapphire arenas of the hills
I was promised an improved infancy.
Sulking, sanctioning the sun,
My memory I left in a ravine,—
Casual louse that tissues the buckwheat,
Aprons rocks, congregates pears
In moonlit bushels
And wakens alleys with a hidden cough.

Dangerously the summer burned
(I had joined the entrainments of the wind.)
. . . .
. . . . but the wind
Died speaking through the ages that you know

And hug, chimney-sooted heart of man!
So was I turned about and back, much as your smoke
Compiles a too well-known biography.

The evening was a spear in the ravine
That throve through a very oak. And had I walked
The dozen particular decimals of time?
Touching an opening laurel, I found
A thief beneath, my stolen book in hand.

"Why are you back here—smiling an iron coffin?"
"To argue with the laurel," I replied:
"Am I justified in transience, fleeing
Under the constant wonder of your eyes—."

He closed the book. And from the Ptolemies
Sand troughed us in a glittering abyss.
A serpent swam a vertex to the sun
—On unpaced beaches leaned its tongue and drummed.
What fountains did I hear? what icy speeches?
Memory, committed to the page, had broke.

FIRST READING

In the beginning Edenic description, the senses mix, for the sound of the sea penetrates the listener's hearing, crossing over the land in exactly the place where he observes the tree to rend the sky. That splitting effect seems to sharpen the hearing, as if indeed the wood of some cedar prow[3] had carved into the stuff of the sky and into the poetic consciousness, the sound of the water passing by means of this vessel in a true transport of the senses. Crane's text is centered as much on sight as on sound,[4] for already at the beginning, the eye is twice stressed, phonetically and still more vigorously by its juxtaposition with the rhyming "sky": "I heard the sea. . ./ I was promised. . . ."

Thrice also the phonetic marker of poetic sight is heard: "*ce*dar," "*sea*," "infan*cy*," so that the seeing, the seer, and the early scene are present even in this auditory passage. In a new infancy, promised as the sapphire sea sets up its theatrical arena among the Mediterranean hills, into which the color of the sea and sky has so clearly mingled, a recreated unicity of childhood would indeed include sight within hearing, as the senses are clarified and merged.

But the speaker is "turned about and back" in his own passage, as a boat might be, after the initial passing of the cedar prow, with the dying of the wind, at the *turn* of the poem. The tree is pierced once again by the evening's lance, thrusting into the oak. Cedar, oak, and laurel, all thrive in the poem's wood, signaled by the initial leaf. The passage is both spatial—as was the initial crossing of the ship and of the sea into the listening land—and temporal, like that of the wind elevating the poet's breath, animating the ages. Evening and ravine remembered pass thriving into the tree, "that throve through very oak." Even the word is sharp as the driving of the spear: some legendary and remembered Siegfried may be summoned to remove the dagger from the natural object split open, or perhaps from a written one, like Bonnefoy's *Pierre écrite.*[5] Passing through the long evening of vigil and of night to make his epic gesture, the speaker then questions the passage along with the moment passing: "And had I walked/ The dozen particular decimals of time?" Here the gesture is only potential: no real or figured Siegfried will pull the dagger from out the tree.

And at the turn of the poem, the wind will die down under the heavy force of the ages, its transparency succumbing to the soot and smoke, although the clear space of the poem itself stretches from sun to sun. On then to the next day's sand, that glittering abyss under the sun for a fresh and final baptism. Here the laurel does not crown a triumph of a completed task, but rather and only the beginning, a tree spreading open until the leaves of the book lie closed on legend as on life.

So the sun washes and bleaches out the memory imprisoned now forever in the pages of the book purloined and self-purloined, stolen from experience, and whose leaves lie idle like a ship becalmed, as the end passes back to the threshold division at the inception, as in a path parted by that initial prow, thriving through the page.

SECOND READING

A re-reading of this passage in the light of another provides yet another path in the reader's mind. Valéry's "Cimetière marin" appeared four years before this poem of Crane's was written: Crane might have seen translated passages or heard of it through his friend Yvor Winters,[6] or sensed its intention in the Provençal landscape in which both poems are steeped. The actual exterior source matters little for the interior passage of the mind. Therein the two poems echo mutually to each other like steps "not lost," "pas perdus" along the corridor of reading stretching between two perceptions.

High noon on the southern coast dazzles upon the sea palpitating between the pines of Valéry's text, in whose grid of leaves the water is caught. Memory reposes in the calmest of abysses, awaiting some rejuvenated and rejuvenating experience, a rebaptism by a waking water. But so far the flat sparkle of the surface is still: "Midi le juste y compose des feux/ La mer" ["Noon the just composes there, from fires,/ The sea"]. The traditional purity of the vision is a mirror for the mind and yet its opposition, as in Mallarmé, Valéry's master: "Ce midi que notre double/ Inconscience approfondit" ["This noon our double/ Unawareness deepens"]. Resisting human change and the defections of time as well as the flaws of human memory, the *glass* of this watching sea suggests self-study as it predicts nonbeing. In Crane's smoke, Valéry's aroma of nothingness blows heavy: "Je hume ici ma future fumée" ["Here I sniff my future smoke"].

Now the examination of Crane's own "Passage" facing the glass of that other poem, each mirroring each, guides this second look.

A reinterpretation may yield the key to some heretofore locked page, like the promise of an "improved infancy" through reading. Valéry's high noon contains in itself quite as surely as does midnight the potentiality of all Crane's "dozen particular decimals of time," just as the opening laurel of immortality debates with transience and the feeling of uselessness under a constant watching eye:

> *Eau sourcilleuse, Oeil qui gardes en toi*
> *Tant de sommeil sous un voile de flamme,*
> *O mon silence! . . .*
>
> Supercilious deep, Eye keeping your secret
> Of all that slumber in a veil of flame,
> Oh my silence! . . .

The eyes belong first to the sun on this sea freshly seen, so far the presumed stealer of the text, the sea whose glittering and unremembering perfection seems to will into silence even the most garrulous book. "Beau ciel, vrai ciel, regarde-moi qui change!" ["Clear sky, true sky, look at my changing!"]

In the phonetic and visual superposition of "Eau/Oeil/O," linking water to eye to exclamation,[7] making visible the stressed and liquid substance of the text, the closure is prepared. For the sea's motion is covered by its roof, glazed by a pitiless luminosity, and closed, like the book's cover, by the thieving sea, stealer of life and of the living body:

> *Je te soutiens, admirable justice*
> *De la lumière aux armes sans pitié!*
>
> I withstand you, admirable justice
> Of light with pitiless weapons

The sand sifts over human transience, trackless and traceless, unremembering and unvital. The force of the reading has died with the wind.

But a mythological creature arises, from the sibilants or from the sand alone, in the hiss and undulation of the S-shaped line:

> *La scintillation sereine sème*
> *Sur l'altitude un dédain souverain*

> The serene scintillation over the height
> Sows a sovereign disdain

One serpentine line ensnares another; witness the stunning triple S of Crane's fifth line: "Sulking, sanctioning the sun,/." So the serpent will pass from sea to sky, in yet another S, thrice shaping the intertextual passage: "A serpent swam a vertex to the sun." This vertex is vertiginous like Valéry's Hydra of life reborn. The wind will lift again its spirit, the waves will break upon these dazzling pages, rifled by the breeze, its pages now freed from the tomb of that unmoving perfection: the rifling of the book is a true metaphor of reading as a steal.

And at last, some mysterious fountain in Crane's poem, like a fountain of life and of poetry, breaks positively into the icy waste, unlike that other imprisoning lake for some long-ago swan, a "cygne"/"signe" marking the place where the wind of the word had once died down. Memory now set loose to be renewed by life is liberated under the sun, in the rising wind resurrected, and sweeps into the rejoicing wave, thrusting both against Crane's iron coffin and Valéry's deadly tranquil roof, toward a more vital passage to be read:

> *Le vent se lève . . . il faut tenter de vivre!*
> *L'air immense ouvre et referme mon livre,*
> *Envolez-vous, pages tout éblouies!*
> *Rompez, vagues! Rompez d'eaux réjouies*
> *Ce toit tranquille où picoraient des focs!*

> The wind is rising: . . . We must try to live!
> The immense air opens and closes my book again,
> Dazzled pages, take your flight!
> Break, waves, break joyously upon
> That tranquil roof where sails were pecking![8]

For the new epic to break into life, the causal and imperfect memory must be left behind with its sickly cough, the opposite of poetry's most vigorous breath. And so the great wind of the word, echoing from the "ère" of ages to the air, lifts in honor of renewed life, breaking into ice and tomb like a wave of "improved" and childlike memory, rebaptised now in the open sea with its possibilities freshly displayed.

Crane's book is closed, his path has "turned about," and the inspiriting wind formerly sensed may have subsided; his poem is written in the past tense. Valéry's sea air opens and closes the book once more, until the wind lifts in the imperative, lifting the spirit with it: the final break here, supremely positive, blowing freshly on Crane's own passage. The last line fits back upon the beginning tree caught against the sky, forming a circular frame visible to those remembering the book but also the breakers, as the rising and full word of wind turns leaf and page in this deeply self-reflective spectacle of the sea. This last turn of the re-reading, then, points the literary passenger's way from the privileged sight of that sea and of that seeing toward the inner seen.

II. SURREALISM AND ITS ARCHITEXTURE
Reading Backwards

THE POETICS OF A SURREALIST PASSAGE

Pour moi, je l'avoue, ces pas sont tout.
For me, I admit, these steps are everything.
ANDRÉ BRETON, *Nadja*

SHADOW

Over present French poetry and poetic theory there hangs the shadow of all past conceptions and realizations—but in particular, those of what is called the heroic period of surrealism. Already the term "heroic" indicates the distance we have come; having left behind our heroes, we have abandoned the epic such as surrealism knew it, represented by such texts as *L'Homme approximatif* [*Approximate Man*] of Tristan Tzara, or André Breton's *Fata Morgana* [Morgan le Fay]. All those larger-than-lifesize gestures, disputes, and manifestoes, to be declaimed in the loudest of voices, indicate an energy no longer visible: take, for example, Breton's magnificent haughty statement in *Le Surréalisme et la peinture* [*Surrealism and Painting*]: "Du sentiment hautain de notre discontinuité . . . nous avons la faiblesse de déduire que nous valons mieux que ce pour quoi nous passons" ["From the lofty feeling of our not fitting in . . . we like to deduce the fact that we are more valuable than that for which we pass"][1] and, in the same volume, his dramatic assessment of the risk and the grandeur of art: "Il n'est pas de grande expédition, en art, qui ne s'entreprenne au péril de la vie . . ." ["there is no great expedition in art which is not undertaken at the peril of life itself . . . ," SP, 204].

Which of our present poets would make it his profession as a preserver of the true faith—that is, the faith in the freedom of the individual act—to spit at passing clergy, as Benjamin Péret did? Whatever feelings he or she might have would be unlikely to find expression in such a manner; it would seem merely silly. And which of our writers would take upon himself the moralistic role of André Breton, excoriating and excommunicating those who seem tempted by journalism or by, just as grave for him, classical meter? One could remark simply on a change of *tone*—but to say no more than that is already to acknowledge, in the clearest possible manner, the distance from surrealism.

Our age cannot revive for itself the epic, the haughty manifesto, or even the grand gesture, whether heroic or mock-heroic. Exactly those scenes most moving in their retelling are marked, set apart so that they cannot be appropriated or recreated. Artaud, "Artaud-le-Momo," removed from the asylum, as if on self-trial, unable to speak intelligibly, scattering his papers across the theater and mouthing his anguished syllables before his listeners, themselves horrified, shamed, and shaken: his gesture cannot be imitated, their shame cannot be shared. Desnos, assaulting his friends in the fury of his hypnotized sleeps: the scene seems true, even if the gesture was exaggerated and the sleep feigned, but it cannot be restaged. The tone of an epoch is surely unmistakable; transposed until it rings false, a changed pitch can mar an entire discourse, an assumed attitude can invalidate a whole way of being.

So the passage chosen here will not lead by way of manifesto and epic gestures or history re-created, but simply by way of texts. Poetry may speak louder than direct affirmation. In the following train-passage from Breton's *Fata Morgana*, the simplest terms indicate the surrealist attitude as surely as the ear-catching rhetoric of the manifestoes:

La petite place qui fuit entourée d'arbres qui diffèrent imperceptiblement de tous les autres
Existe pour que nous la traversions sous tel angle dans la vraie vie
Le ruisseau en cette boucle même comme en nulle autre de tous les ruisseaux
Est maître d'un secret qu'il ne peut faire nôtre à la volée
Derrière la fenêtre celle-ci faiblement lumineuse entre bien d'autres plus ou moins lumineuses
Ce qui se passe

Est de toute importance pour nous peut-être faudrait-il revenir
Avoir le courage de sonner

. . .

Et pourtant je suis sûr qu'au fond du bois fermé à clé qui tourne en ce moment contre la vitre
S'ouvre la seule clairière

The little square fleeing, surrounded by trees imperceptibly different from all others
Exists for us to cross it at a certain angle in real life
The stream in this very curve as in no other among the streams
Has hold of a secret it can't reveal in such a rush
Behind this window faintly luminous among many others more or less luminous
What *happens*
Is all-important for us perhaps we should turn back
Have the courage to ring

. . .

And yet I'm sure that in the locked depths of the forest turning right now against the window
The only clearing opens[2]

Breton clearly believes in the destined passage: the little square is to be the privileged place of crossing, with some special significance given to the happenings "de toute importance pour nous," wherein the italicization of "se passe" clearly marks an essential *passage*. Despite the popular conception of surrealism as the rejection of untransformed reality, he maintains his enthusiastic belief in the actual, for the angular crossing is situated "dans la vraie vie." The heart of his poetics is a defense of the passionate and the unique, as they are interdependent for him and for surrealism. Behind this landscape, the reader hears Breton's self-questioning in *Nadja*, where he wonders "of what unique message I was the bearer, answering for it with my life." What is not questioned is the singularity of things and their messages. These trees, seen from a train, are unlike all others; the bend in the river differs; the passionate event is for "us" but not for all; and as if by *chance*, and also by destiny (or the latter in guise of the former), the clearing opens unique within the forest formerly locked shut. That this certainty should be shadowed by an indefinite fear not only effects a contrast in poetic terms, but announces the unrest underlying even the great statement of "Amour fou," where the haunting continues: "It would still be possible to turn back."[3] Against the vagueness of the "perhaps," applying only to the action, the perception of the unique remains unchallenged; the passionate is seen as passing, yet essential, as in the Baudelairean attitude toward the woman loved all the more for being only a passerby.

In his last essays, Breton maintains his faith in a unique fate, the perception of which is singled out by objective chance, coinciding with our innermost desire. Speaking of the stones in the Lot River near his house of which no persons would ever select the same ones, he states the underlying principle of the personal unique: "Tant il est vrai qu'on ne trouve que ce dont on éprouve en profondeur le besoin . . ." ["So true is it that one finds only what one feels the deepest need for . . ."]. This concealed desire is, in fact, "the diamond within us. . . ." Almost forty years earlier, in *Le Surréalisme et la peinture*, he was already speaking of this power of recognition as the primary component of sentient existence. The sensory verbs, he said then, must not be conjugated like the others: the *déjà vu*, or what we think we have seen before, the *déjà entendu* or what we think we have heard before, are to be recognized as extraordinary in their uniqueness and their recurrence. "Voir, entendre, n'est rien. Reconnaître, (ou ne pas reconnaître) est tout. Entre ce que je reconnais et ce que je ne reconnais pas il y a moi. Et ce que je ne reconnais pas, je continuerai à ne pas le reconnaître" ["Seeing, hearing, is nothing at all. Recognizing (or not recognizing) is everything. Between what I recognize and what I do not recognize there is myself. And what I do not recognize, I shall continue not to recognize," SP, 66]. It is as if the recognition or the refusal of recognition were itself to be chosen, as one chooses being, once and for all. The object seen or comprehended, is selected because it is known *again*, rather than becoming known; this, like love, happens "always for the first time."

In the text it was perhaps to be a question of *going back* ("Peut-être faudrait-il revenir . . ."). I would maintain that the surrealist (an adjective I would oppose to the "surrealistic," that watered-down, meek, and totally inappropriate form) lies exactly and implicitly in this recurrence, which, however, takes place for the first time, illogically and—some would say therefore—poetically. Along with this lack of a certain beginning, or, in Derridian terms, this lack of an origin, goes the lack of an end, as in Breton's claim to like only "unfinished things." The figure of surrealism is turned always toward the future, in a state of expectancy: Breton's transformation of François Villon's line: "Where are the snows of yesteryear?" into these snows yet to come, "Where are the snows of tomorrow?" is of primary significance. The congruence of a *not yet* and an *already* makes available and unforgettable an entire presence in its delirium ("délire de la présence absolue," AF, 85)[3] and is the key to the tensions by which surrealist poetry is, often precariously, balanced. What Breton chooses to recognize or not to recognize is itself the key to his own theories and his own imaginative fields, *La Clé des champs*. The key to the closed forest of this text is perhaps simply the belief in an absolute and a unique presence: if we could open some door to some enchanted garden, then. . . . The nostalgia of the past event, "once upon a time," and a firm faith in the always-to-come, these two become indistinguishable in the surrealist marvelous.

But it may be the play of the most somber uncertainty and unrest against the positive manifesto tone ("we declare") that makes the language of surrealism of such appeal to our own age of breach and rupture. The following anguished text is taken from *L' Amour fou*, and it succeeds directly an interrogation of some absolute presence, in a moment of privilege, of epiphany, vision, and choice, then countered:

Je vois le mal et le bien dans leur état brut, le mal l'emportant de toute la facilité de la souffrance. . . . La vie est lente et l'homme ne sait guère la jouer. . . . Qui m'accompagne, qui me précède cette nuit encore une fois? . . . Il serait encore temps de reculer.

I see evil and good in their raw state, evil winning out with all the ease of suffering. . . . Life is slow, and man hardly knows how to play it. . . . Who goes with me, who precedes me again once more tonight? . . . It would still be possible to turn back. (AF 85)

The distance from this turning back to the other more hopeful one is tragically clear. Yet Breton did not turn back; the title chosen for his essays posthumously published indicates his spirit as determinedly positive: *Perspective cavalière*.[4] The ambivalent force of the surrealist inquiry remains nevertheless the most lasting for us. "Of what am I finally capable?" Breton asked himself. In *Nadja*, *L'Amour fou*, and *Arcane 17*, the penetration of this doubt and the ironic clarity of this opposition between the sure and the uncertain, the heroic and the questioning, reaches heights of poetic spirit that Breton's "poems" (of which he was not very proud) could never reach. These passages are the primary subject of study here.

OPENING PASSAGE

If the surrealist passage in general is of particular interest to us, it is because the psychological reality of change corresponds to textual metaphors of opening and doubling: communicating vessels, swinging doors, half-open windows, where the clash between two complementary elements gives full play to metamorphosis. The privileged space of *play* is set apart by the initial entry into the poem, and its being perceived.

The openings of surrealist poems repay careful attention as self-conscious thresholds of perception. Here, for instance, the speaker or dreamer may initiate the discourse by announcing the entrance into an utterly different state, as in the following openings of three poems of extraordinary vision, Breton's "Je rêve je te vois superposée" ["I dream I see you superimposed"], Eluard's "J'ai rêvé que j'ai marché vite" ["I dreamed I walked quickly"], and Desnos's "J'ai rêvé tellement de toi . . ." ["I have dreamed so much of you"]. Or again, emptying out of space and its replenishing may set off the poem, as in Eluard's "Tout se vide et se remplit . . ." ["Everything is voided and fills up again . . ."]. Among the diverse fashions of marking this space *apart*, the most dramatic is that of burning. The space lying outside or, in a correspondence between spatial and temporal terms frequently signaled, the space lying before that of the textual experience is burned away by the explicit wish of the speaker, or by the intimate juxtaposition of his vision with that burning as in Eluard's line: "Je vois brûler l'eau pure et l'herbe du matin" ["I see the pure water burning and the morning grass"].[5]

No case of opening is clearer than in Breton's poem "Vigilance," which might form the center of any discourse on surrealist dream and vision as they are consumed. The action is set off within a dream, uncompromising in regard to ordinary space. Vigilance is kept precisely against the "normal" human consent to living, so that the dream serves for a meditation on meditation. Here the sun's rays have the singular precision of a mountain's profile, while the rain blossoms, flowering outward in all directions with the fragrance of hawthorn, like a Proustian memory lingering: "Je vois les arêtes du soleil/ À travers l'aubépine de la pluie" ["I see the bones of the sun/ Through the hawthorn of the rain," P, 103–4]. The prepositional "à travers," "through" or "across" carries the reader over to the other side of normal perception, indicating an extraordinary passage into the space of surrealist perception, and its easy flux. The guiding grammatical thread causes the poet and reader to cross through one state to the next, as if in a labyrinth lit at last, by a *fil conducteur* that is no gift of Ariadne, but is rather a chosen passage.

THE COVERED PASSAGE

In the surrealist vision, the present object passes into other present and absent objects, the possible into other possibles: the letters *Mazda* advertising the light bulb and written in neon illuminate in Breton's mind the letters *Nadja*, the name of the one luminously mad to the extreme, for whom a dark window becomes red even before the light appears inside. But at this distance from the movement, the reader may prefer to follow the visually ambivalent invitation that Breton proffers in *Les Vases communicants* [*Communicating Vessels*]: "The flagrant passage of the eyes. . . ."[6]

Now there may be covered passages in the most apparently innocent texts, even the most open of them. We have only to look at Aragon's suggestive menace: "Je vais vous décrire si vous n'êtes *pas sages*" ["I am going to describe you if you are not good"], he threatens, so that our description depends on our own comportment and wisdom, "sages" or "pas sages," permitted the *pas-sage* or not. "Passage de l'Opéra onirique" ["Passage of the Oneiric Opera," or the dream works] reads the sign over Aragon's arcade, where the wise and privileged passerby celebrates the wonders of tomorrow being born "from the ruins of today's mysteries."[7] Mystery, like love, attaches to transience: if Breton refuses to enter the room described by Dostoievski because of its essential nullity or dullness, Aragon's arcade is already attractive to the *être de passage*. This arcade is the perfect expression of the lyric comportment by which Breton defines surrealism's attitude, which, like a life, is made up of "the series of steps, shorter or longer, but marvelous," the series permitted to the man "unchained"; for the surrealist reader liberated from reason as from tradition, "these *steps* are everything." It is of them that Nadja will speak, optimistically; "Les Pas perdus? Mais il n'y en a pas" ["Lost Steps? There aren't any," N, 82].

In *Anicet ou le panorama, roman*, the hero's steps take him into the Passage des Cosmoramas, compared to a magician's box in which worlds themselves are transformed. In the cosmic text of passage and panorama, the false lighting from the glass roof conflicts with the interior lights to permit "all error and all interpretations," the essential ambivalence basic to surrealist poetry's openness. Half-open to the day and yet half-closed, dim and duplicitous, attractive and anguishing, the passage resembles a great glass coffin—not so unlike Marcel Duchamp's *Large Glass*, where the bride is buried to herself as she is stripped bare "by her bachelors, even"—the passage unsettles, rendering strange the familiar. The "threshold between sky and earth" that is the glass roof encourages a further play on that glass as *vers*, as the verse permits light to pass through and to transform the assemblage of diverse objects and letters, in this undersea world of shop signs and ambiguous indications. "*Je suis le passage*," says the narrator, at once being (*être*) and following (*suivre*) the transforming corridor, as on a stage; as the sign for the lamp is seen to change from Mazda to Nadja, so also do perceptions change.

As with Arthur Rimbaud's "great disorientation in all time and space" that the surrealists advocate, the covered passage is marked for Aragon by an absence of authorial and perceptual control. In his essay on the *Incipit*, he claims to have chosen the Passage de l'Opéra as his guiding image because his description would soon be unverifiable, the destruction of the passage being imminent.[8] So the passage is sometimes devoted to its own undoing, showing a determinedly mobile architexture, and not an unchangeable, monumental architecture, finished and perfected. Texts, like possibilities, are to be left open.

"ONE IN THE OTHER": Communicating Images

Flamme d'eau guide-moi jusqu'à la mer de feu.
Flame of water guide me to the sea of fire.
ANDRÉ BRETON, *"Sur la route qui monte et qui descend"*[1]

In its title alone, the surrealist game of "the one in the other" indicates one of the principal attitudes of the movement and its imagination; the fluidity of the latter facilitates the multiple movement and transpositions of poetic images as they pass each into the next and the techniques of anamorphosis and paronomasis, those plays of double vision as of double meaning producing a sort of two-faced text. The attitude suggests also a flexibility of reading, which the following pages would like to exemplify.

How does one element pass into another, and how can this passage illustrate what I intend by a poetics of passage? In homage to Gaston Bachelard,[2] the philosopher of surrealism as he was called, and in reference to his studies of the elements, and also in homage to the baroque imagery with which surrealism is so imbued, I will attempt to sketch here the fluidity of a few exemplary elemental texts, as a partial model for poetic metamorphosis.

The following section extends the metaphor of passage, and the images or techniques connected with it, to the surrealist and postsurrealist poem in particular: surrealism lends itself especially well to such a setting of the stage, based as it is on notions of flux and metamorphosis. Of all the elements, water is the one associated with flux, and the source of metaphoric fruitfulness: the most extreme transpositions of related images illustrate the living flow of this privileged element.

This study might begin with a principle resembling that of Anaxagoras: there is in everything a portion of everything. As for the surrealist game alluded to, it illustrates the general rule of the mental process by which we pass from one element to the second, which is already contained potentially in the first, for instance, in Breton's celebrated example of the lion's mane contained in the candle flame by its redness and fury: thus, the lion is included in the candle, and vice versa.

Along the length of this corridor composed of surrealist texts, water and fire will be seen to respond and correspond at each step of the passage. The initial word will often appear to determine the concluding word, as if the text were constructing itself while going from one end to the other, thus producing an architecture in textual motion, or an architexture to which the reader must contribute. (It is taken for granted, let me say at the start, that the passage made or taken by any reader can be concerned with but few of the many possible senses, since it will bring to light certain spots and hide others.)

The texts chosen here represent each a different architexture of passage; the first, that of Eluard, begins with crystallized water as it leads toward a fountain, rapidly moving from solid to liquid, while passing through a fiery danger. In the second, that of Desnos, fire serving as guide to the dream for the mermaid, the figure whose image constantly haunts Desnos, comes from the depths of the ocean to which it returns. In the final example, Breton's invocation of the wild and watery flame, running the course of the text until a final confluence with the sea of fire, itself exemplifies the communicating elements making up the complementary pair, inseparable at last one from the other, water and flame, fire and sea. The alchemists could not have dreamed a one-in-the-other more perfect than this.[3] In the matrix-fire, now equivalent to the water-womb, one element produces the other, by which in turn it is contained for a new gestation.

FLAME AND FOUNTAIN: ELUARD

Le diamant qui'il ne t'a pas donné c'est parce qu'il l'a eu à la fin de sa vie, il n'en connaissait plus la musique, il ne pouvait plus le lancer en l'air, il avait perdu l'illu-

sion du soleil, il ne voyait plus la pierre de ta nudité, chaton de cette bague tournée vers toi.

De l'arabesque qui fermait les lieux d'ivresse, la ronce douce, squelette de ton pouce et tous ces signes précurseurs de retour de flamme ta grâce de la Sainte-Claire. Dans les lieux d'ivresse, la bourrasque de palmes et de vin noir fait rage. Les figures dentelées du jugement d'hier conservent aux journées leurs heures entrouvertes. Es-tu sûre, héroïne aux sens de phare, d'avoir vaincu la miséricorde et l'ombre, ces deux soeurs lavandières, le monde se détachera bien assez vite de leur crinière peignant l'encens sur le bord des fontaines.

The diamond he did not give you it was because he had it at the end of his life, when he no longer knew its music, could no longer toss it in the air, had lost the illusion of the sun, no longer saw the stone of your nakedness, the jewel of this ring turned toward you.

Of the arabesque closing the inebriating places, the gentle thorn, skeleton of your thumb, and all these signs as the precursors of the flame's return, you Saint-Claire gracefulness. In the inebriating places the gustiness of palms and black wine rages. The lacy figures of yesterday's judgment keep in the days their half-opened hours. Are you sure, heroine with lighthouse senses, of having vanquished pity and shadow, those two washersisters? The world will detach itself soon enough from their mane of hair as it paints incense on the rim of fountains.

("Nouveaux Poèmes," *Capitale de la douleur,* 1926)

Eluard's poem suggests itself as a path leading from a first hard jewel to a liquid diamond: the rim of the fountain finally visible resembles the circle of a ring in which the *water* of the jewel is set. A more discreet jewel than those so delightfully described by Denis Diderot,[4] this ring still can be imagined to direct its rays toward the fountains to induce their talkativeness heard throughout the preceding text; thus the magic stone opens the privileged place of intoxication through a correspondence of diamantine matter. Since these "lieux d'ivresse" are protected by a charm, the obstacle must be overcome, the taboo transgressed for the would-be heroine to arrive within. It is time for a new religion, after deliverance from the ancient ritual symbolized by the incense marking the rim of the fountains. The exact verb used is, in fact, "détacher" ("le monde se détachera"), phonetically permitting the unspotting of the old as well as the liberation of the new. Thus the clear may merge with the free, to celebrate the joining of jewel and fountain, of magic force and deep refreshment.

The first paragraph indicates age by a quadrupled negative series: "n'a pas donné," "ne connaissait plus," "ne pouvait plus," "ne voyait plus," contrasting with the single positive expression "il l'a eu." This last is the absolute contrary of Eluard's famous ambiguous title, "Donner avoir," whose two senses are equally positive: the first and most obvious, suggesting a generosity profitable to the giver; and the second, "donner à voir," suggesting a vision offered. Here, on the contrary, the feeling is wholly pessimistic: the negated items constitute an important series of losses, that of music, of beauty, of lightness, of the sun and its illumination of what might once have been a transfigured beauty. The deprivation of these items seems quite as major as that of the "pierre de ta nudité," lost through a kind of blindness, in contrast to the vision preceding and following.

In the second paragraph, the images of diamond and of transparent water pass into the grace and gracefulness of the Saint-Claire fountain. But this privileged place to celebrate vision—where the most sparkling of waters is imbibed—is closed off by the gentle arabesque of the blackberry's brambles, made sweeter still by the implied fruit. The "ronce douce" makes a sweetly deceptive curve that casually strips skin and flesh from bone, leaving only the skeleton of a thumb, as a mockery of the sign of unction. Now the searing red cruelty of blood and other violent signs summon the flame, as if the animal thirsted for any liquid whatever. How should we dare to drink from even the most graceful well protected in such fashion?

In the final paragraph, the water darkens, the fountain returns to its drunken virtue, filling up with wine-dark strength corresponding to the deepening red of the bruise as it is seen to "ripen," the source now considered a wounding of the earth. Unsurprisingly, then, the graceful arabesque of bramble is convulsed by a wild flurry of wind-swept palms, as the silence changes to storm. The heroine, whose watery grace has already been threatened by a fiery animality, retains her radiance even through a phonetic implication of artificiality: "phare/fard," the latter resonance recalling Mallarmé and the clown's "fard" removed by the water in which he plunges.[5] But the tables are turned doubly, in the reversal of images we have come to associate with the baroque sensibility,[6] as the cosmetic of "fard"—usually the explicit covering—is given only an interior resonance within the obvious illumination of the "phare," and the washing is attributed to other beings, these two dark sisters of the past, pity and shadow, whose tears wash but neither refresh nor clarify.[7] Here the reader may remember Tzara's violent Dada diatribe against the humility of regret and against pity as the "chocolate in the veins of all men," the block to all those crystalline corridors (equivalent to the fountains in the present poem), the obstacle to all the clear and rapid hurtling of so many verbal volcanoes down the slope of a poetry set free.[8] The last syllable of "lavand*ière*" brings yet one more echo of the past, an "hier" as in the preceding sentence: "jugement d'hier," a reference all the more phonetically charged as those figures were said to protect the "heures entrou*vertes*," thus again as water preserves the green ("vert") of growing things. But again in reverse, it is of these washerwomen, ordinarily those who remove the stains or "taches" of use, that the world will detach or unspot itself.

Like sirens only implicit, they only implicitly comb their hair: "crinière peignant," for here again the words apply their second sense, painting the incense like a protective shield and sign around the edge of the fountain as upon the rim of a well. It is from that *mark* and from all past emblems that the poem is finally to be washed clean, at its new source. And despite the heavy perfume of ritual incense threatening to close once more the circle of water like a ring (a taboo all the more powerful for its joining of perfume with water in a secret liquid correspondence), language still moves in the direction of a pagan drunkenness, of a water virgin, free, and joyously unsaved. From the former sign, which would have marked the fountain as a celebration of the past, and from the "fard," both implicit stains, the text detaches itself, refreshed.

It is evident at last that the previously unoffered diamond, with all its repressed energy, will surge forth like a fountain into the passage of the poem. The water is newly opened, and the text is posed on the edge, "sur le bord," like the surrealist moment itself, in voluntary risk and positive renewal.

FLAME AND COAL: DESNOS

. . .

La belle nageuse qui avait peur du corail ce matin s'éveille
Le corail couronné de houx frappe à sa porte
Ah! encore le charbon toujours le charbon
Je t'en conjure charbon génie tutélaire du rêve et de ma solitude laisse-moi
laisse-moi parler encore de la belle nageuse qui avait peur du corail
Ne tyrannise plus ce séduisant sujet de mes rêves
La belle nageuse reposait dans un lit de dentelles et d'oiseaux
Les vêtements sur une chaise au pied du lit étaient illuminés par les lueurs
les dernières lueurs de charbon
Celui-ci venu des profondeurs du ciel de la terre et de la mer était fier de
son bec de corail et de ses grandes ailes de crêpe

. . .

Mais la nageuse elle-même s'est rendormie
Et je reste face à face avec le feu et je resterai la nuit durant à interroger le
charbon aux ailes de ténèbres qui persiste à projeter sur mon chemin
monotone l'ombre de ses fumées et le reflet terrible de ses braises
Charbon sonore charbon impitoyable charbon

. . .

The lovely swimmer who feared the coral this morning awakes
The coral crowned with holly knocks at her door
Ah, the coal again always the coal
I beg you coal tutelary genius of the dream and of my solitude
let me let me speak again of the lovely swimmer
who feared the coral
Tyrannize this seductive subject of my dreams no longer
The lovely swimmer rested in a bed of lace and birds
Her clothes on a chair at the foot of the bed were lit by
the glimmers the last glimmers of coal
Come from the depths of sky and earth and sea the coal took
great pride in its coral beak and in its great crepe wings

. . .

But the swimmer herself has gone back to sleep

And I remain face to face with the fire and I shall remain the night long questioning the coal with shadow wings who persists in casting over my monotonous path the shade of its smoke and the terrible reflection of its embers
Coal resounding coal merciless coal

("*L'Identité des images*," 1927)

Desnos's poem "L'Identité des images"[9] places in a typically tentative equilibrium of subtle interconnections the elements of water, fire, and earth. In his texts the interruption of the voyage is marked by the disappearance of the figure representing the sea, that is, the mermaid. (Mélusine has rather a different form here from the one that she assumes in *Arcane 17*, for instance; we might just as soon speak of *la soeur ennemie* as of a *soror* and mistress.) Here the voyage begins with water, that element identified with the beautiful swimmer, whose double is the coral, bearing a parallel relation to the flame, prefiguring it by its color the embers. Since the ember contains its own potential charring, and since, freed from the dull fulminations of logic against retrospectivity, the ember contains the coal from which it came, one still within the other, the coral contains also, within its flame, its coal, like the mermaid, her ocean. Now the coal, black as the earth from which it comes, presents a coral beak and wings of crepe, thus combining red and black, life and mourning, and trembles in the air like a leaf almost consumed, while still ardent to the extreme. The text, like its image and no less rapidly consumed, bedecks itself in jewels of jet and ruby, always with a delicacy translated by the lace and feathers of the bed where the swimmer lies like the lightest of dreaming corpses on the most ethereal of funeral pyres.

In a further step, the feather bed (for each swimmer is not only mermaid but princess) suggests a celestial creature just descended birdlike from the sky to earth, whereas the swimmer recently come forth from the water and implicated in her own fireside dreaming, responds on behalf of sea and fire. Seduction is double within this wavering light: Appearing to enchant the poet, the swimmer is nonetheless herself enchanted by the image of the embers casting their redness on the clothing removed, and on the bed of lace and feathers, sailing like a ship transporting swimmer and reader as if on birdwing. If the fire serves as guiding light for the dream, the black of mourning echoes the sailors perished in the shipwrecks caused by the mermaid, in this dream turned nightmare, by the coal itself risen from off the ships. The bed turns to cemetery as the dream risks a devalorisation of its mystery.

For it is finally to the blackness of coal that the once vital and now dying colors are reduced: "Charbon sonore charbon impitoyable charbon." From the initial sonorous description, the golden color ("son or") is fading, for the black of coal absorbs the softness of the gold, as the Byzantine blaze dies down. If the surrealist poem is alchemical work, in which the basest and barest matter is transmuted into the gold and crystal of all poetry, the loss is a grave one, like a voluntary passage made, then feared, mocked, and finally denied. The sonorous possibilities of the alluring mermaid song are reduced to the mere whistling of a domestic kettle, psychologically tame after the seductive dreams of the night. Compare the reduction with the remarkable passage in Desnos's late and dreary novel of 1943, *Le Vin est tiré*, celebrating the healthy morning coffee after the excesses of the corrupt, drugged, and drunken night, and imagine the distance from Baudelaire's magnificent celebration of intoxicants in his prose poem on the subject: "Enivrez-vous, de vin, de vertu, de poésie, à votre guise . . ." ["Get drunk on wine, on virtue, on poetry, as you choose. . ."]. If the real and actual are eventually to be opposed to the dream, as Desnos seems to have it, then the tragic passing from red fire and golden sonority to black is perhaps inevitable, even as the elements are implied in each other.

FLAME AND SEA: BRETON

Dîtes-moi où s'arrêtera la flamme
Existe-t-il un signalement des flammes
Celle-ci corne à peine le papier
Elle se cache dans les fleurs et rien ne l'alimente

. . .

Et la flamme court toujours

. . .

Mais la flamme elle ne saurait reprendre haleine
Malheur à une flamme qui reprendrait haleine
Je pense à une flamme barbare
Comme celle qui passant dans ce restaurant de nuit brûle aux doigts des femmes les éventails
Comme celle qui marche à toute heure sur ma trace
Et luit à la tombée des feuilles dans chaque feuille qui tombe
Flamme d'eau guide-moi jusqu'à la mer de feu

Tell me where the flame will stop
Is there a signaling of flames?
This one scarcely singes the paper's corner
It hides among the flowers and nothing feeds it

. . .

And the flame runs still

. . .

But the flame could not catch its breath
Woe to the flame which would catch its breath
I think of a barbaric flame
Like the one passing in this night restaurant burning the women's fans in their fingers
Like the one following me at every moment
And gleaming at leaf-fall in each falling leaf
Flame of water guide me to the sea of fire

("*Sur la route qui monte et qui descend*")
(pp. 76–79)

Breton's "Route qui monte et qui descend" frames itself by the imperative mode at its outset and its end, an energetic setting for the racing flame and uninterrupted text, quite unlike the textual voyages of Desnos always halted by ice floes or a mermaid. Aragon's early "perpetual motion" (*Le Mouvement perpétuel*, reads one of his titles), leads to this interminable path with its marking question, pointing to its own meaning or an absence: "Existe-t-il un signalement des flammes?" The question is itself singled out and pointed to by the insistent repetition: "flamme . . . flamme . . . flamme."

The direction is characterized by its ambiguity, for the water, sought out as the complement to the flame, finally merges its flood with the fire. But already at the outset the question is posed: What will be the end of this fiery text? The fire, unnourished, scarcely burns, so that the paper is only faintly traced by the visit which hardly turns down the corner of the card. The ardent passage leads across hemisphere, precipice, and ocean, in search of other signals just as empty of precise content, equally dry of matter:

Lorsque les signaux tournent au bord des voies avec un bruit sec
Qui ressemble à ce craquement spécial sous les pas des prêtres

When the signals spin at the edge of ways with a dry sound
Like the odd creaking of a priest's step (p. 77)

The way up and down includes both earth and sea, hill and wave, as well as the signals pointed toward its own signaling.

In particular the flame-hair, this double medusa, doubles as a "méduse" or jellyfish whose long tentacle streamers burn and enfever, and a Gorgon whose serpentine locks stream or undulate wavelike, so that this "jolie rousse" with Pre-Raphaelite hair is ardor itself and also wave, *onde* from which any *ondine* might issue;

Et cette chevelure qui ne s'attarde point à se défaire
Flotte sur l'air médusé C'est la flamme
Méfiez-vous elle profanerait votre tombe

And this hair not long in its undoing
Floats on the medusa air It's the flame
Careful it might profane your tomb [p. 78]

"Elle profanerait votre tombe . . .": Like another cemetery by the sea, this tomb also is visited by the wings of Valéry's doves. It will find its exact contrary in a green rebirth in the same poem, in a hope-filled origin: "Dans le premier berceau de feuillage la flamme tombe" ["In the first crib of foliage the flame falls," p. 78]. Wings and leaves recur in the fan held by the woman seated at her water mirror in Breton's poem "Je rêve je te vois superposée," where the comb takes on wing-shape.

The polite, even bourgeois, settings of restaurant and of civilized gesture, are still traversed poetically by the barbaric wildness of the flames until the final junction, where implied tomb ("La tombée des feuilles dans chaque feuille qui tombe") and falling leaf ("tombe/tomber") form a model of this brief study, of its own leaves in their passage, falling one onto the other.

After the preliminary study of surrealism as a movement and of these three complementary and elementary texts, the following chapters will celebrate further rites of the surrealist passage, and of its elements ("Rites of a Flowing Element"), and from one time to the next ("Ode to a Surrealist Baroque"). The flow of these parts themselves should in some sense reflect the interior architexture, both ardent and in flux, centered on the metaphoric passage as a vital center: "I have not left the place . . .," says Aragon's Anicet (A, 49).

RITES OF A FLOWING ELEMENT
From Surrealism to Paz and Merrill

The preceding section considered the structure of three surrealist passages, themselves concerned with the passage of elements into each other. Now according to an ideal poetics of passage, the poem would be seen as a framed section, with stable boundaries, but permitting a flow between the images and elements as between the communicating vessels in the metaphor privileged by Breton. The poem would be both a set piece and a representation of flux, a microcosm where the privileged place and moment are bordered and yet open, where the works can be publicly performed and yet be a private inner experience, both participating in the initiatory rite of passage as it is or played out.

With regard to framing, the surrealist poem of passage often *sets* its events in another place or moment from those of the reader or the narrator, or then places them at a certain distance from the events and figures contained in everyday life; for instance, the expression "over there" ("là-bas") of the entrance to Breton's poem analyzed here, "On me dit que là-bas . . ." ["They tell me that over there . . ."], is equivalent to the primary positioned "there" of James Merrill's "Mad Scene," "There I saw the cloud-clot." The unfamiliar personages opening Desnos's poem "Paroles des rochers," "La reine de l'azur et le fou du vide passent dans un cab" ["The queen of azure and the fool of emptiness pass in a coach"] and Paz's geographically peculiar initial comparison, "Como la marejada verde de marzo en el campo" ["Like the green March surf in the field,"] serve in the same way to isolate each poem's experience from the here and now and the persons peopling our days. Whether the initial scene concerns dreams or daydreams, it is thus distanced from the factual present by its poetic fiction and the faraway character of its frame.

Some ideal conditions in which the metamorphosis proper to what can be roughly called the surrealist poem can prosper have been discussed in the first and second essays of this section. They will be illustrated here by four examples: two from major surrealists and two from among the surrealist successors, Octavio Paz and James Merrill, who have unquestionably retained at its peak the spirit of openness and of optimal flux. The point here is not to make a further analysis of the spirit of surrealism itself; rather, the examples are chosen to demonstrate certain ways the reader may perceive a flow-in-the-text.

The liminal consciousness, once developed, may enhance the sensitivity to ends of texts; that is, to the state of crossing-over from within the poem to without and vice versa. Often the entrance or exit of a surrealist text may be strongly marked as closing off the beginnings and endings of ritual space, either by the setting of a fire, as in Breton's poem "Vigilance," already mentioned, by the traditional and celebratory spilling of blood upon the threshold, or by the arranging of hair, a well-known ritual of passage. Desnos's poem "L'Idée fixe," (DP, 114–115), incantatory and obsessive, is exactly centered on the haunting image of the woman's hair resembling a hand, as if the poet's own touch were to be transposed upon it: "Mais tes cheveux si bien nattés ont la forme d'une main" ["But your hair, so neatly braided, has the form of a hand"] ends the poem, which also begins with this fixation on and of the hair and this manual obsession. The poem by Desnos considered here has also a capillary concern, is written in salute of the manes of hair waving in the night, serving as the instruments of passage to a beach scene, as *wave to wave*; the equivalent is that of the praise to blonde hair, "Éloge du blond" in the *Paysan de Paris* ending as it does, after some properly serpentine twists, by a permanent or Marcelle wave, these undulations meeting the others, in this flowing passage. All the texts here share a watery baptism.

The concept of ritual space is responsible for yet another noticeable trait: the narrator is frequently the observer rather than the actor in the scene to whom the speech or the vision is attributed.

For instance: in Desnos's speaking hair, "'A bientôt,' disent les chevelures" ["'See you soon,' says the hair"]; or in Breton's attribution of the source of landscape lighting to the viewer, "Quel est donc ce pays lointain/Qui semble tirer toute sa lumière de ta vie?" ["What distant country is this/Which seems to take all its light from your life?"]; or in his recounting of a legend told, "On me dit que là-bas . . .". Despite their being attributed to another voice or gesture or perception, these acts and views are kept in deliberately sharp and narrow focus, just at the edge of the eyelashes in Breton's poem ("à la pointe de tes cils") or by a formal narrowing of the phrase "nothing but" in Paz, "No hay nada sino . . . ." Such specificity of imagination is fruitful for surrealist poetry, whether it is exemplified within the dream, the narration, or the comparison.

Finally, an extensive play of contraries is often seen to announce the central metamorphosis. Thus, in the Breton poem under consideration, black is opposed to white and crow to snow; in the text of Paz, clothed to unclothed; in that of Merrill, bibs to shrouds; and in that of Desnos, human loneliness to the crowded object world. Desnos above all manifests a double sensitivity to such contraries as night and day, dream and real: "J'ai tant rêvé de toi" ["I have dreamed of you so much"] begins Desnos's most famous poem (untitled, DP, 95), and the visual and mental combat between light and a dream or the real and the shadow, or the world of dawn or day and that of night, compose the threshold setting for many of his masterpieces of surrealist chiaroscuro. Even more than the other surrealists, Desnos shows in the beginnings, the conclusions, and even the titles of his poems a particular concern with liminality and with bordering; his extreme fascination with the figures of day and night can easily be seen in a few of his titles: "Vent nocturne" ["Night Wind"]; "Les Espaces du sommeil" ["The Spaces of Sleep"]; "Le Suicidé de nuit" ["The Night Suicide"]; "Il fait nuit" ["It Is Night"]; "The Night of Loveless Nights" (whose title, originally in English, repeats the obsession); "Les Sources de la nuit" ["The Fountains of Night"]; and "Enfin sortir de la nuit" ["To Leave Night at Last"], for instance. Or "Pour un rêve de jour" ["For a Dream of Daylight"]; "Au petit jour" ["At Dawn"]; "Chanson du petit jour" ["Song of Dawn"]. Or then, marked by both, "Un Jour qu'il faisait nuit" ["One Day When It Was Night"].

"Pour un rêve de jour" ["For a Dream in Day," DP, 130-31] has as its central figure a sphinx noiselessly ascending and descending a stair, while the "Spaces of Sleep" ["Les Espaces du Sommeil"] are marked by a central presence, as are those of waking: "Dans la nuit il y a toi . . . dans le jour aussi" ["In the night you are there . . . in the day too," DP, 96-7]. Desnos's celebrated war poetry is inscribed under the heading "State of Watchfulness" ["État de veille," Robert Gedet, 1943], and his best poetry might be thought of as fitting at once under that state and in the sleep spaces. His most notable characters are also figures of a double world or a double sensitivity: the mermaid singing in the fire encountered in the preceding essay, since any mermaid is already liminal by her nature; and the wanderers in *La Liberté ou l'amour!* (*Freedom or Love!*), Louise Lame and the Corsair Sanglot, the Blade and the Sob, with male and female rôles reversed even in their names.

Parallel to these semantic and visual oppositions (of light and dark, naked and clothed, and so on), a series of crucial shifts and crossings back and forth from one element to another, of the sort illustrated in the preceding essay, form an ambivalent threshold, the propitious context for one key shift or major turn. This in turn leads toward a final metamorphosis or crossing, whether one way or two. This latter "turn" is the essential twist to the text, or the swerve in the act(s) of the poem. As for the exit threshold in the poems discussed here, the construction is variously conceived: noticeably heavy, for instance, at the exit of the Desnos poem "Identité des images," poured forth in one rush through the frenzied length of the fourth from last line, with the intensity directed toward the final image, thus announced. Typography stresses the final threshold of the Breton poem, where the capital letters of "D'APRÈS" herald the ending image; a similar isolation is seen in the concluding line of the Paz poem, and in the sudden brevity of the visual exit from Merrill's "Mad Scene." The reading of these thresholds for entrance and exit reveals the technical brilliance of the surrealist hand seen even in passing, unsurpassed at every turn.

The following examples from surrealism and after illustrate the play and interplay of images, within the overall setting found by a liquid imagination: the metamorphic facility supposes, even imposes, a receptivity to flux and flow on the part of the reader. The reading calls for a heightened sensibility to that passage marked by shifts and turns, whose current requires the liquid element. The first of the two following surrealist poems illustrates sound and sight play, and the second, the play of structures—from Breton to Desnos the distance is great, and the readings are different of necessity. Yet to those two examples of surrealist water poetry, in its potential for *passage* as the term is used here, respond the Paz and Merrill poems placed after them, element matching element and summit matching summit.

ANDRÉ BRETON: "ON ME DIT QUE LÀ-BAS . . ."

On me dit que là-bas les plages sont noires
De la lave allée à la mer
Et se déroulent au pied d'un immense pic fumant de neige
Sous un second soleil de serins sauvages
Quel est donc ce pays lointain
Qui semble tirer toute sa lumière de ta vie
Il tremble bien réel à la pointe de tes cils
Doux à ta carnation comme un linge immatériel
Frais sorti de la malle entr'ouverte des âges
Derrière toi
Lançant ses derniers feux sombres entre tes jambes
Le sol du paradis perdu
Glace de ténèbres miroir d'amour
Et plus bas vers tes bras qui s'ouvrent
A la preuve par le printemps
D'APRÈS
De l'inexistence du mal
Tout le pommier en fleur de la mer

They tell me that over there the beaches are black
With lava gone to the sea
And unfurl at the foot of a great peak smoking with snow
Under a second sun of wild canaries
What is this distant country then
Which seems to draw all its light from your life
It trembles real at the tip of your lashes
Sweet as an immaterial linen to your carnation
Freshly drawn from the half-open trunk of ages
Behind you
Casting its last somber fires between your legs
Ground of the lost paradise
Glass of shadows mirror of love
And lower toward your arms opening
To the proof by spring
OF AFTERWARDS
Of evil's not existing
All the flowering appletree of the sea

Breton's poem exemplifies a passage not only from an outer landscape to an imagined and interior one, but also from a state of doubt and a tone of wonder to a direct and certain statement, with a parallel transposition and expansion. The threshold or initial scene is removed from the space of the actual by its deliberate invocation of hearsay: "On me dit que . . . ." There is no claim of knowing or even of caring, and the vague "là-bas" serves only to intensify that first impersonal disclaimer of responsibility: "On me dit . . . ." Not only is the scene that of legend, but the narrator is, so to speak, off-screen, not implicated in the text, which is itself set quite simply somewhere toward the sea.

Nor is there any initial claim to a unique environment: we recognize the blackness of the beaches as part of standard surrealist discourse, precisely since they are the exact opposite of the white beaches of tradition and of cliché. If Noah's ark were re-created, says Breton, he would like the crow to return in place of the dove. The further play of contraries takes similar lines: the volcano's smoking peak gives off a white cloud like snow, this fire and this freezing forming a space, privileged because paradoxical, for the marvelous. The hiss of boiling lava and the seething of waves are formally caught in the sibilants of the fourth line, "*s*ous un *s*econd *s*oleil de *s*erins *s*auvages," as the molten waters singe the beach or then the *page* always implicit in those *plages*.

The one addressed fills the passage with her own vision, from which the future soon may issue, the poem's birth coeval with the birth of a landscape. The country of the distant and lost paradise still remains distinct from the actually seen, is marked as possible if uncertain, certainly as unique, by its vacillation and its focus directly before the eyes: "il tremble bien réel à la pointe de tes cils." History shines somber but pure, erotic but veiled, for the trunk as the specific material repository of historical events and future predictions lies at present only partly agape, like the swinging doors and the communicating vessels of surrealist thought, already mentioned: images of closure and containers partially sealed from the outside, partially open within. In particular, the informing male force is hidden, or at least half-hidden, present only by phonetic implication as if stowed away within the expression of and in the trunk itself, "la malle" where "le mâle" is concealed, and later then in the evil ["le mal"] ruled nonexistent by the poetic law of renaissance.[1] The terms reflect each other in their play and flow, just as the two mirror images are seen to do: the "glace de ténèbres" and the "miroir d'amour" responding as one sense of "glace" responds to the others, *glace* to *glace*, mirror to glass to ice as, in the poem, supposition flows into reality and implied vision into explicit love. In the same way, the term "soleil" has prepared the ardent ground for the "sol," which half-echoes it, just as the "glace" and the "miroir" share a mutual meaning, and just as the terms "malle" and "mal" lie half-open to the phonetically implicit force of the "mâle." Thus form and image reflect upon each other, inside the limits of the frame, or of the mirror. The third image, that of the trunk, works its transformation in the poem itself, revealing the arms beneath and opening the text downward to an exactly inverted space. The complex play of multiple reflections develops the flux of the poem, now flowing past the time of hearsay, fiction, and legend, triumphant into the moment of poetic truth, both reflective and reflexive, a passage by the mirror and the eye.

Yet fire calls forth fire as well as ice: the smoking peak majestically summons the somber flames of an heretofore absent sun, finally reborn in the season of the text, in the springtime after the time of loss. As the temporal and salutary motif is stressed, AFTERWARDS so the Fall and the memory or history of its former power for future condemnation is denied; the second sun re-creates the lost paradise, and the appletree no longer bears a lethal fruit, suggesting the sin of prideful knowledge, but instead a bloom opening now, to expand into a wider element, this passage spreading from the land outward into the ocean, free of limit. The entire poem exists toward this crossing out, extends from a hope held initially and by others ["on . . ."], at a distance, to the poetically possible intimate fusion of the land and the sea, in a double incursion. Finally this other privileged vision, trembling at lash-end, is the source of a mirror's own reflection. The waves flower at last within the appletree renascent in the present of the text, as the boughs stretch out into the sea, one in the other now forever.

The passing of the pages heard unfolding in the roll of ocean along the beach, "Les pages . . . se déroulent,"—where the play and flow of "page"/"plage" are constant—is also a flowering outward, as the seer ["à la pointe de tes cils"] and the hearer ["on me dit"] unite and are transcended by their own vision and listening. The reading passes from lava to leaves, from volcano to earth, from earth to sea, again and marvelously in flower after its hissing confrontation with the blackness of beaches, fire seething against water.

The poem expands and bridges one element with the other as it moves from its liminal uncertainty to the surest final synthesis: its conclusion is not, like its opening, the legend of a distance recounted, but the intimacy of a presence. Baudelaire's own incursion here, as his *Flowers of Evil* merge with those flowers of good seen afterwards, complicates the texture and redeems the Fall.

ROBERT DESNOS: "PAROLES DES ROCHERS"

La reine de l'azur et le fou du vide passent dans un cab
A chaque fenêtre s'accoudent les chevelures
Et les chevelures disent: "A bientôt!"
"A bientôt!" disent les méduses
"A bientôt!" disent les soies
Disent les nacres disent les perles disent les diamants
A bientôt une nuit des nuits sans lune et sans étoile
Une nuit de tous les littorals et de toutes les forêts
Une nuit de tout amour et de toute éternité
Une vitre se fend à la fenêtre guettée
Une étoffe claque sur la campagne tragique
Tu seras seul
Parmi les débris de nacre et les diamants carbonisés
Les perles mortes
Seul parmi les soies qui auront été des robes vidées à ton approche
Parmi les sillages de méduses enfuies quand ton regard s'est levé
Seules peut-être les chevelures ne fuiront pas
T'obéiront
Fléchiront dans tes doigts comme d'irrévocables condamnations
Chevelures courtes des filles qui m'aimèrent
Chevelures longues des femmes qui m'aimèrent
Et que je n'aimai pas
Restez longtemps aux fenêtres chevelures!
Une nuit de toutes les nuits du littoral
Une nuit de lustre et de funérailles
Un escalier se déroule sous mes pas et la nuit et le jour ne révèlent à mon destin que ténèbres et échecs
L'immense colonne de marbre le doute soutient seule le ciel sur ma tête
Les bouteilles vides dont j'écrase le verre en tessons éclatants
Le parfum du liège abandonné par la mer
Les filets des bateaux imaginés par les petites filles
Les débris de la nacre qui se pulvérise lentement
Un soir de tous les soirs d'amour et d'éternité

L'infini profond douleur désir poésie amour révélation miracle révolution amour l'infini profond m'enveloppe de ténèbres bavardes
Les infinis éternels se brisent en tessons ô chevelure!
C'était ce sera une nuit des nuits sans lune ni perle
Sans même de bouteilles brisées.

The queen of the azure and the fool of emptiness pass by in a coach
Heads of hair at every window
And the hair says "See you soon!"
"See you soon!" say the jellyfish
"See you soon!" say the silks
Says the mother-of-pearl, say the pearls, say the diamonds
Soon a night of nights without moon and without star
A night of all the coasts and all the forests
A night of all love and all eternity
A pane cracks in the watched window
A piece of cloth flaps over the tragic countryside
You will be alone
Among the ruins of mother-of-pearl and the carbonized diamonds
The dead pearls
Alone among the silks which will have been dresses emptied at your approach
Among the tracks of the jellyfish fled when your glance was raised
Only perhaps the heads of hair will not disappear
Will obey you
Will give way in your fingers like irrevocable condemnations
Short hair of girls who loved me
Long hair of women who loved me
And whom I did not love
Linger long at the windows, heads of hair!
A night of all the nights of the coast
A night of lustre and of funerals.
A staircase is spread out beneath my steps and night and day only reveal shadows and failures to my fate

The vast marble column doubt alone holds up the sky above my
  head
The empty bottles whose glass I crush into dazzling shards
The scent of cork thrown up by the sea
The nets of boats imagined by little girls
The ruins of mother-of-pearl slowly grinding itself to powder
An evening of all the evenings of love and eternity
Deep infinity grief desire poetry love revelation miracle revolution
  love deep infinity surrounds me with talkative shadows
The eternal infinities are broken in shards O head of hair!
It was it will be a night of nights without moon or pearl
Without even broken bottles

Desnos's poem also concerns poet and watery scene, but its development depends on reduction rather than on expansion, as the poem moves toward a turning in rather than out: not a crossing-over, not an extension or an expansion, but an inward passage.

The initial catalog is formed of three triplets, beginning with the cry from the windows thrice repeated, where a possible link between elements might be posited as follows: from hair to the mythical figure of the Medusa, herself equipped with streaming hair, *méduse* being also the name for jellyfish. Thus the hair streaming in the water is seen to strike the reader with wonder, that is, to mesmerize or to *méduser*. So the silk of the hair is inextricably tied to the reader's wonder, perhaps, at the luxury of the text.

Once this kind of link is observed, it may be seen to provide an inner microstructure parallel to the outer or macrostructure. For example, the chorus of precious objects is linked by substance as surely as the first noisy triplet is linked in form; the silk of the hair suggests the luxury of mother-of-pearl, the very expression already containing the substance, the luxurious pearl, paralleled by the equal luxury of the diamond. Finally, the third triplet, beginning by the same phrase of ambivalent farewell, "à bientôt," which links the whole tripartite construction, is formed of three lines, each a description of night, with two modifiers for each line: without moon and without stars (cliché items here negativized), but deeply nocturnal, taking into itself the dark spaces of all the coasts and all the forests. Two concrete items are rendered all-inclusive and finally, with the intensity of love and eternity, both are made complete: "tout amour" and "toute éternité" (two abstractions both particular and holistic). These introductory items neatly fitting into each other, in a tightly structured catalog of cumulative effect, return in the body of the poem in various elaborations and are given differing emotional weights, yet are finally shattered asunder as the poem moves or flows past the individual elements of its original setting.

A brief sketch of the structure may suffice for this passing glance. Images of separation and tragedy come forward each by each, as they appear to the lonely poet in his seaside vision. A pane of glass cracks in two, like a premonition of the future bottle that will be broken into shards at the poem's end. A cloth rag flaps sadly, clacking in the wind like a hollow mockery of a flag or of a sail over a countryside where no allegiance and no departure are possible, so that flag or sail is useless. The solitude of the poet ["tu seras seul"] is itself triply mirrored in the images surrounding "alone" among the debris of that same mother-of-pearl already present, and the same diamonds denatured, having become opaque, and the same pearls now lustreless, in the hopeless ruin of each formerly luxurious element. Alone among the silks, themselves once the signs of luxury like the long hair, these materials are now emptied at the mere sound of his footsteps, which frighten away even the jellyfish. Yet the hair, deprived of its silkiness, stripped of its rich medusa metaphor, may remain in the lonely night. And there the third "seul" in its two readings: "alone" and "only" changes, with a hint of irony, to a possible positive after the negative repetition of "seul . . . seul."[2] "Seules peut-être les chevelures ne fuiront pas." Retained with the hair is the whole tradition of beauty saluted in the poetry of love and the setting of the spectacular: "Restez longtemps aux fenêtres chevelures!"

Finally the night regains its ultimate dominion, responding to the poet's aloneness, while its shadows—later said to be at the source of all poetry—nourish the poet's own tenebral language, its "infini profond douleur désir." Such an exalted nocturnal setting affects even the chandelier of stars, its own luster invaded already by the gloom of failure. The glass fragments and the mother-of-pearl now disintegrated into powder remain as desolate traces on the shore abandoned by the sea, as the talkative shadows, in their endless whispering, tease the poet before whom even the infinite flow of discourse[3] is marked by discontinuity. The precious objects and the gleaming stage props desert the darkness, taking with them even the tracks and traces, these in a final negative triplet summoning back by implication the powerful repetition: "alone . . . alone . . . alone" ["Seul . . . seul . . . seules."] It is as if the whole vision were finally denied in a surprise and upset ending, typical of Desnos, whose passage is often most complex when it seems simplest, diminishing at just the expected point of summation, in a constant self-undoing.

Eluard once asked, in a title, as if to stress the question itself: "La Jarre peut-elle être plus belle que l'eau?" ["Can the Jar Be Lovelier than the Water?"] That the transparent container of so much of Desnos's own mythology, the bottle[4] as the source of song and mermaid, of poetic message and lyric intoxication, should here be denied even in its fragments, may be interpreted either as the end of singing or then as the possibility of cosmic rebirth, after this night "of loveless nights," in its dark passage.

OCTAVIO PAZ: "COMO LA MAREJADA . . ."

The Breton poem ends with a "flowering appletree of the sea," thus a transposition from land to water: Rimbaud's poem "Marine" comes to mind, in which the masts of sailing ships are perceived amid the wheat fields. In Paz's comparison, "Como la marejada," the green waves are continued and stressed by the phonetic repetition "*mar*ejada . . . *mar*zo,"[5] that is, by the early spring of the countryside, and then make their rolling passage across the fields of the text, opening the way to the joint fertility of land and sea. The same kind of mutual play and fertilizing imagery is often stressed in the verbal interchange between "plages" and "pages," the beaches bringing from their ocean border their liquid offerings to the pale sterility of the paper, making their own watery passage.

Como la marejada verde de marzo en el campo
Entre los años de sequía te abres paso
Nuestras miradas se cruzan se entrelazan
Tejen un transparente vestido de fuego
Una yedra dorada que te cubre
Alta y desnuda sonries como la catedral el día del incendio
Con el mismo gesto de la lluvia en el trópico lo has arrasado todo
Los dias harapientos caen a nuestros pies
No hay nada sino dos seres desnudos y abrazados
Un surtidor en el centro de la pieza
Manantiales que duermen con los ojos abiertos
Jardines de agua flores de agua piedras preciosas de agua
Verdes monarquías

La noche de jade gira lentamente sobre si misma

Like the green March surf in the field
Between the desiccated years you make your way
Our looks cross embrace
Weave a transparent cloth of fire
A gilded ivy to cover you
Tall and bare you smile like the cathedral on the day of
conflagration
With the very gesture of rain in the tropics you have cleared it all
away
The days fall ragged at our feet
There is nothing but two beings bare embracing
A fountain in the room's center
Springs at their sources sleeping open-eyed
Gardens of water flowers of water precious stones of water
Green monarchies

The night of jade spins slowly upon itself

This vision is in part the product of "our" exchanged looks: "nuestra mirada," passing between the narrator and his loved one, between writer and reader, or then text and observer. The transparent garment woven by the glance is here said to be of fire and also of ivy, for an ardent, even inflammatory text and a time-consecrated tissue of supports indicated by the verb "tejen," stressing the very weaving of the text.

As the surf rolls against the desiccation, covering it over while opening the way to future fruition, so the descriptions of elements covered and discovered alternate: "transparente" / "te cubre" / "desnuda" / "harapientos" / "desnudos." Like a photograph seen flickering through a window shade, the "transparente" is seen in another and still another form, in a repeated stressing of the bare. The basic image of transparency guides the reading toward the triplet of water images, after the initial source in the sea. "Lluvia," "surtidor," and "manantiales," bring the freshness of rain, fountain, and spring toward the second triplet, condensed into one line: "agua . . . agua . . . agua . . . ," with its gradual intensification and hardening into the jewels of water, supremely valorized. The last have been themselves prepared by the word "transparente" as a noun, being the stained glass window that is a metonymy for the cathedral, to whose mellowed walls the ivy may cling, as to a time-honored text; through its prism of colors we look again at all the hues, especially at nature's green in the "marejada verde," extending its vital color to the ivy and the liquid "verdes monarquías."[6] The latter's richness is appropriate to the value of the jewels and to the revivifying force of the water, as the two senses of "precious" reach their climax in the black green night, where finally the *jade* of the spinning world mirrors and transforms the initial "mare*jada*," heightening its green and concentrating its fertility in a renewed intensity, like a jeweled microcosm of nature's rebirth.

In Breton's poem "On me dit que là-bas," the expression APRÈS qualifies as a temporal arrest, setting apart the remainder of the poem; similarly, in Paz's poem the isolation of the last line and the adverbial expression "lentamente" make a dramatic ritardando for the ring of jade turning in tranquil darkness, after the transparent day. From naked morning and clarity under a March sun to the slow cycling of the green night, the person addressed has opened a transparent path, so that the sea might wash away all that is irrelevant to prepare the final and fertile revolution of the poem as it turns upon itself, the jade cycle of the diurnal and nocturnal transparent perhaps only to the watchfulness of those who sleep "open eyed."

JAMES MERRILL: "THE MAD SCENE"

The cycle of James Merrill's poem is different from all the preceding ones. As with much contemporary American poetry variously called open, bare, minimal or naked, the strength of the text comes precisely from the unassuming character of the guiding image. A poem about a laundry cycle fits in wonderful incongruity against the "mad scene" from *Lucia di Lammermoor*, intertwined with it and lending credibility to the final notes of the flute and the mordent. Here, when one might expect a burst into song, nature bursts instead into grief: the progression is no less moving than it would be in a loftier setting for what is seen.

THE MAD SCENE

Again last night I dreamed the dream called Laundry.
In it, the sheets and towels of a life we were going to share,
The milk-stiff bibs, the shroud, each rag to be ever
Trampled or soiled, bled on or groped for blindly,
Came swooning out of an enormous willow hamper
Onto moon-marbly boards. We had just met. I watched
From outer darkness. I had dressed myself in clothes
Of new fiber that never stains or wrinkles, never
Wears thin. The opera house sparkled with tiers
And tiers of eyes, like mine enlarged by belladonna,
Trained inward. There I saw the cloud-clot, gust by gust,
Form, and the lightning bite, and the roan mane unloosen.
Fingers were running in panic over the flute's nine gates.

Why did I flinch? I loved you. And in the downpour laughed
To see us wrung white, gnarled together, one
Topmost mordent of wisteria,
As the lean tree burst into grief.

Like many surrealist poems, this one is set off by its dream narration, and by an announcement of repetition: "Again last night." Like Breton's celebrated text beginning "Toujours pour la première fois," the opening here combines freshness and sameness, as if in an initial and initiatory rite of passage, often repeated and all the more efficacious for being so. The setting of the familiar dream even includes a title, as if the specific and recurring vision were accorded a category unto itself. Whether the other dreams have their own titles or not, this one is unique, as a spectacle to be observed ["I watched"], like the opera included within it, a new twist on the play within the play, a *mise-en-abyme* of the seen within the scene.

The instantly presented play of oppositions provides density and drama to the dream passage: all the numberless and colorless sheets and towels of indistinct domestic sharing are heaped into the hamper with the telltale rags bearing their small dramas, stained by the offshoots of love ["milk-stiff bibs"] followed then by the equally stiffened ends of life ["shrouds"]. For the milk joins birth to rigid death, cleverly and with no less pain and no uncertain irony, as the word "stiff" with its erotic asides predicts the corpse and the rigid blood-stained sheets "bled on or groped for blindly." Just so, the "swoon" implies equally a cadaver (shrouded in the negative sense) and the opposite image of a nightgown, a positive shroud for a sort of lovesick swooning. Lucia here may be sung by Joan Sutherland, whose roan mane is "unloosed. . . ." The latter implication prepares the "moon-marbly" boards of a sentimental spectacle, just as it picks up on the bibs, rather less sentimental: a romantic night, the moonlit scene set for the theater, and the hamper serving to contain what has been used of life and to offer costumes. The ironic double containment serves as a *hamper* or impediment to passion and as an eventual source of refreshment, a picnic basket but also a humble guardian for those inevitable bibs, with their ineradicable reminder of what must be refreshed, of the double cycle of life and death, and of laundry.

The essential of the tale is embedded in the text, which affirms the recent starting point of whatever passion there had been—"We had just met"—so that the fresh beginning of refreshment redeems the repetition of the setting—"Again last night." The central body of the poem is built around the verbs of seeing and nonperception, from the negative expression "groped for blindly" to the isolating statement of the narrator's perception as an outsider to his own dream, "I watched," and the series of eyes leading to the still-distanced "There I saw." The observer observes, presumably protected from both birth and death, bib and shroud, like a modern man in a white suit—a new fiber not to be bled on, trampled, or soiled, a suit in which not to be involved. But that garment, just another costume, will in the long run or the read cycle not prove impervious after all to gnarling and ringing, to passion or to grief.

The eyes of the reader, trained as they are on the narrator's own and on their enlargement as they sparkle in the darkness, are, again like his, trained in their vision inward in several senses: trained by this poem and the experience it forces upon all watchers, trained for dreaming, and trained also on to the inner spectacle with a focus on Form. The word "form" works as a noun—"I saw Form"—and as a verb—"I saw the cloud-clot form, like blood." The violence of this formation picks up the "bled on" and the "soiled," prepares the bite of lightning and the quasi-variant, "mordent," as if the latter were a metamorphosis from "mordant" in another spelling, a shift, different in color and tone, from another wash and its own *lye.*

The crucial shifts from form to form, idea to idea are clearly marked: grammatical and psychological, from the word "ever" positive in form to the doubled "never never" in its almost hysterical refusal; phonetic and semantic, from the "tiers" prepared for spectacle to the tears in the eyes, whose effect is all the greater after the half-bitter laughter during the downpour (the rinse cycle as it prepares the final grief). Irony informs the dream, as well as the poem, for it is after all only a question of a laundry cycle; the mechanical wringing has only a psychological import, beyond its overtly musical ring befitting the mordent. The wisteria bears an initial sound akin also to wistfulness, and the splendid isolation of the term "one" after the word "together" mocks all loving union. Hesitations and ambiguities abound in the reading "Why did I flinch?" he asks. "Because I loved you," or even: "Why did I flinch, since I loved you?" The laughter is motivated and forced by the irony, and by the sadness into which the tree bursts, in place of the awaited song, as this melancholy replaces spring, expectant green by real pallor, "wrung white," suddenly dry even of tears.

The final lines are accented by their stark brevity, contrasting with the other fifteen lines of the spectacle, which have led to this "one topmost mordent," this slight twist and this severe "leanness" of the anguished tree, the natural image now replacing the cultural one, leaves after clothes. The neutrally presented dream with its colorless title shifts to the hysterical wringing, by implication partly musical (for instance, the ringing of bells); partly psychological and physical (the wringing of hands, as if the actor were gnarled by age and suffering); but the beginning is young, always starting "again." The pain is now prepared by the five stark monosyllables and their sudden interruption before the final and terrible monosyllabic "grief" sufficiently announced only by the tears. On this final transforming image, then, the key to the poem makes its turn.

From the domestic to the dramatic to the musical, from the personal to the natural, the scene is always heavily charged with emotion, to which the narrator, in his white vestment, is not immune. He watches, but also weeps and laughs, finally transferring his apprehensiveness about his clothing, that previous noninvolvement suggested by his avoiding "stains and wrinkles and tatters," to a tree. When it bursts into sadness as a singer bursts into song, or a tree into "leaf," the rhyme prepares implicitly the deception and the surprise: the grief bears the weight and the charge of the whole poem, the emotional force of which is expected at the end of the cycle. Here one image crosses over into another, in a green cycling reminiscent of Paz but at the same time a recycling, by liquid metamorphosis and gradual intensification, from the simple announcement of dream into the final exchange that gives the game away, as tragic. *Green trees burst into leaf, but these lean trees burst into grief;*[8] as the appletree may flower in the sea, or ships sail among the wheat, so does one word pass, like one image or one concept, into another, "l'un dans l'autre" forever flowing and forever merged.

While not systematic, the changes rung in all these poems are nevertheless mutually illuminating in their collective resonance of necessity subjectively perceived. The reader whose eye has been trained in and trained on surrealism—although not necessarily a watery eye—discerns a privileged element as the truest place for a text of passage. The corridor of underwater lighting open to day and to dark, the arcade seen as a magician's metamorphic cabinet, provides both a walk around, an excursion, and the threshold of an endless traversal or incursion, a transfer or crossing at once mental, spatial, and temporal, a moment extended and yet precise. Having learned to celebrate the one in the other,[9] to navigate the liquid crossing of contraries, this stroller of a corridor merges with the swimmer of the text, in all the ambivalence of this most modern myth, which points the way toward a poetics of the passage.

ODE TO A SURREALIST BAROQUE
Scève, Góngora, and Desnos

Tout ici se rencontre et se métamorphose.
Everything meets here and is metamorphosed.
ROBERT DESNOS, "Crépuscule d'été"

The passage by poetic memory is haunting, as the crossing-over of one poet's thought or words into those of another is sometimes conscious, as in the case of the surrealist Desnos's memory of the mannerist and baroque style of Scève and Góngora, and sometimes less so, as in his reflection on Apollinaire, whose figure as traveler presides over the present textual voyage, looking backwards.

Within the "errance" or lyrical wandering of surrealism—where the state of openness and of availability to chance encounters makes a privileged place of the street—Desnos occupies a unique position. It was of his explorations and experiments that Breton often spoke, praising their adventuresome quality,[1] of him that Aragon said, "My friend Robert Desnos, this singular modern sage, who has strange ships in every convolution of his brain" [PP, 112]. And it is an incontestable fact that his poems and his two surrealist novels, the brief and brilliant *Deuil pour deuil* [*Mourning for Mourning*] of 1924 and the more famous *La Liberté ou l'amour!* [*Freedom or Love!*] of 1928,[2] unfold in a setting totally unlike that of any of his contemporaries, reminiscent of nothing so much as what we might call the romantic baroque. The darkest of sleep spaces play against the great clear expanses of street, sea, and desert, and the wanderer in dream or in the historical past is continuous with the adventurer of the landscape presumed to be "real." Almost always, and this is a stylistic trait unique to Desnos, the setting is noticeable for the intensity of contrasts: the one and the many, as exemplified by the lonely walker and the crowd, the traveler and the institution (The Corsair Sanglot and the Boarding School of the Humming-Bird Garden), the single hero and the multiple women leaving their footsteps on the stair; or then, the play of deserted square and city street, island and sea. Or again, and here a memory of Mallarmé's own dark and light: chalk figures on a blackboard like stars against a sky. In particular, the image of an explorer dressed in white, lost in a desert of anthracite coal, combines a stark visual contrast with the familiar romantic topos of the wandering figure; this image initiates the following sentence of expressive contrast: ". . . and he listens, along with the moaning of the wind in the chimney, to the songs of invisible archangels inculcating in him the love of night and the love of the midday sun, uniform, solemn and tragic like the shadows . . ." [LA, 98]. These cast shadows give a depth to Desnos's prose and poetry quite unlike that of any other surrealist.

Parallel to the optically melodramatic opposition of light and dark, each heightened by the other, runs a topological opposition of near to far, and the related contrast of hot to cold: of this sort of contrast the figure of the mermaid is an ubiquitous example, as she represents the convergence of land and water, human and animal. In their lyrical oppositional style, the works of Desnos send us back to the settings of Scève and the lonely wanderings of Góngora quite as much as to Villon and Gérard de Nerval and Rimbaud, his acknowledged heros and predecessors. Of Scève he says nothing, of Góngora a good deal: by a further opposition and encounter, this double path might serve as a reader's own passage, from one age to another, looking backward from modern poetry to that of its ancestors.

SCÈVE'S SETTING

First of all, in this play of contraries, the mark of a school is recognizable: the Petrarchan influence is strong. Within this setting Scève, certainly the most baroque poet of the School of Lyon, seems especially near to the tone and the attitude or the spirit of Desnos. A commentary on either might offer, in the best of circumstances, mutual illumination.

Roughly, the resemblances might be grouped into three categories: the first, that of word play, can be rapidly sketched and cannot be said to be more than the beginning stroke of a deeper line. For instance, a Scève dizain is frequently organized around the permutations of one word:

> *Voulant je veulx que mon si hault vouloir*
> *De son bas vol s'estende à la vollée*
> *Or ce mien vueil ne peult en rien valoir,*
> *Ne la pensée, ainsi comme avolée. . . .*

> Wanting I want my so noble wanting
> With its low flight to stretch high
> Now this my wish can be worth nothing,
> Nor can thought, as it has taken flight . . .[3]

Here the entire poem is based on the various forms of the verb "to want" and its permutations. Any number of examples could be given of this tendency in Desnos, from *P'Oasis*, *Langage cuit* [*Cooked Language*] and *L'Aumonyme* (a convergence of Alms—Aumone—and the Homonym), from which this untranslatable example is taken:

> *En attendant*
> *en nattant l'attente.*
> *Sous quelle tente*
> *mes tantes*
>
> . . .
>
> *En nattant les cheveux du silence*
> *six lances*
> *percent mes pensées en attendant.*[4]

The fact that so many poems of this type exist, proving the poet's consciousness of and attachment to this kind of verbal theatrics, leads to the reader's consciousness of still other possibilities. For instance, the emphasis on the two possible senses of the final word, as it is stressed in Scève's dizain XXIV, might go unnoticed were it not for the sensitivity developed in the reader by the extent of ambivalent play to which the poetic line is subjected:

Quand l'oeil aux champs est d'esclairs esblouy,
Luy semble nuict quelque part, qu'il regarde:
Puis peu à peu de clarté resjouy

. . .

Ne me pers plus en veue coustumière.
Car seulement pour t'adorer je vis.

When the eye is dazzled by flashes in the fields
It seems night to him on every side.
Then little by little he rejoices in the bright

. . .

Lose me no longer in habitual sight.
For only to adore you do I live.

Glimpsed again, in a new light, the last word changes the meaning, by its own anamorphic play: "For only to adore you did I see."[5] Now the poetic eye (and the reader's eye accustomed to that poetically self-reflective gaze) is conscious of just that play of contraries and of just those hidden ambivalencies in the stanzas of Scève and is aware how the corresponding poems and passage of Desnos are constructed on just those double keystones. Both poets excel in the establishment of the *concetto*, which is then the point of the poem as it reflects back, paradoxically and perfectly, upon itself.

And the melodramatic setting, shadows playing against clarities, the tenebral tendency of Scève lit only by the fires of desire, entices the modern reader back from Desnos, for just such contrasts as the following built into the dizain 7: "Quand nasquit celle en qui mourant je vis" ["When she was born in whom I live dying"] and the following lines:

En la clarté de mes desirs funèbres,
Où plus m'allume, et plus, dont m'esmerveille,
Elle m'abysme en profondes ténèbres.

In the brightness of my funeral desires,
Where she lights me still further, and moreover, at which I marvel,
She plunges me abysmally into the deepest shadows.

On the swerving line between sight and nonsight, living and dying, the great style of mannerist quavering is based; a fine example is the following, from Don Carlo Gesualdo:

S'io non miro non moro,
Non mirando non vivo;
Pur morto io son, ne son di vita privo.
O miracol d'amore, ahi, strana sorte,
Che il viver non già vita, e morir morte.

If I behold not, I die not.
Not beholding, I live not.
So I am dead but not bereft of life.
O wonder of love, what strange fate,
Where living is no life, and dying is no death.[6]

The great poems of Desnos on darkness and light: "Pour un rêve de jour," "Il fait nuit," "Vie d'ébène," "Désespoir du soleil," and "Les Espaces du sommeil," are themselves clarified and deepened by the reading of these other plays of dark and light. The baroque illumination against which we should read Desnos can only serve him well.

And finally, in the self-conscious and brilliant artistry of the self-reflective poem, where the burning of a love is also the consuming of the word, where the absence and the presence can be taken to refer also to the text, as can the distant and the near, to the poetic word, Scève and Desnos triumph, among all others, over the possible preciosity of such conceits by the very sensible tragedy of the poetic line. "Near your eyes, I freeze," runs the dizain XXVI, "and in the distance I smoke with ardor"; a volcano may be consumed in one night but the burning of the self-consuming text will not end. (One could also situate the dizains CCCLII and CCCCII, both of which play on the day and dying, the night and burning, along this same passage, to clarify the Desnosian background.) Among the numerous and extensive plays of contraries on which the lyricism of Desnos is based, one passage of absence and presence, of knowing and not knowing, of remembering and forgetting, will serve as a clear parallel to Scève's baroque windings, illustrated in his dizain CCXV:

> *Je m'en absente et tant, et tant de foys,*
> *Qu'en la voyant je la me cuyde absente:*
> *Et si ne puis bonnement toutes foys,*
> *Que, moy absent, elle ne soit présente.*
>
> . . .
>
> *Mais quand alors je la veulx oblier,*
> *M'en souvenant, je m'oblie moymesmes.*

> So many times do I absent myself
> That in seeing her I think her absent from me:
> And thus cannot prevent, all the same,
> That when I am absent, present she is.
>
> . . .
>
> But when I wish then to forget her,
> Remembering her, I forget myself.

"Far from me, oh my present present torment, far from me," reads one of Desnos's most famous poems, "Oh far from me, you are far from me:"

> *Loin de moi et cependant présent à ton insu*
>
> . . .
>
> *Loin de moi,*
> *Si tu savais.*
>
> . . .
>
> *Si tu savais comme le monde m'est soumis.*
> *Et toi, belle insoumise aussi, comme tu es ma prisonnière.*
> *O toi loin de moi, à qui je suis soumis.*
> *Si tu savais.*

> Far from me and yet present without knowing it
>
> . . .
>
> Far from me,
> If you only knew.
>
> . . .

If only you knew how the world submits to me.
And you, lovely unsubmissive one, how you also are my prisoner.
Oh you far from me to whom I submit.
If only you knew. (DP, 99–100)

And finally, in this same *Délie* of Scève, among all the poems that bring so near to us the background of this most contemporary poet, there lies the key, perhaps, to Desnos's last poems, called *Contrée*. After the flashes of surrealism, these poems may seem set pieces. But here too, in these formal rhythms and set models, rigor still makes a place for the tragic and the lyric, within the clash of good and evil, of brightness and dark, of day and night. Amid the lines of Renaissance figuring and baroque twisting, the reader is shown what—knowing or unknowing—he was looking for, the key, now at last, to a whole poetic country:

. . .

Si grand clarté s'est icy demonstrée,
Que quand mes yeulx l'ont soubdain rencontrée,
Ils m'ont perdu au bien, qui seul me nuict.
Car son cler jour serenant la Contrée,
Et ma pensée a mys l'obscure nuict.

Such a great clarity has shown itself here,
That when my eyes suddenly encountered it,
They lost me to the good, which alone harms me.
For its clear day calming the Country,
And my thought has moved the dark night.

Scève's *Contrée* then, from so long ago, provides the poetry of Desnos in its darkly splendid baroque presence among us with its proper light and its just setting: in this country of convergences, distant and near.

THE WANDERER'S WOOD: GÓNGORA TO DESNOS

The self-conscious poetry of Desnos could trace a passage back to other leaves of other books: "Other songs have died in my mouth," says Garcilaso de la Vega, and Desnos sings of poems dead and dried up in his mouth also, leaving only the remains of such trees as used to flourish in his dreams. They turn to straw, and he remains silent:

> *Je n'ai jamais parlé de mon rêve de paille*
> *Mais où sont partis les arbres solitaires du théâtre*
> *Je ne sais où je vais j'ai des feuilles dans la main j'ai des feuilles dans la bouche*
>
> . . .
>
> *J'ai des feuilles dans la main j'ai des feuilles dans la bouche*
>
> . . .
>
> I have never spoken of my dream of straw
> But where have they gone, the solitary trees of the theater
> I know not where I go I've leaves in my hand leaves in my mouth.
>
> . . .
>
> I've leaves in my hand leaves in my mouth. (DP, 150)

But this forest shelters also the path along which Góngora has led to Desnos: Desnos himself speaks of this path and of the field of his poetry, and of the key which Góngora holds to his own domain:

> . . . The poem follows its path in a straight line, through the forest dark and thick, down a great avenue, but on the right and the left, twisting crosswise paths head out toward the limits: Góngora suppresses none of this, he absorbs it all, keeps it with him, carries it off like a prisoner pursued, who would take along with him the fields themselves and not only their key.[7]

Góngora, the "angel de las tinieblas" and Desnos the poet of shadows also, of *Les Ténèbres* and "Les Profondeurs de la nuit," and of *The Night of Loveless Nights*—these two poets of darkness are companions along the road traced here, in its baroque setting and its modern passage. Góngora's Galatea prepares Desnos's "Nymphe Calixto," and even Desnos's "Nymphe prétexte, Calixto," when in his last poems, written with *Contrée* in 1942 and 1943, just before his death, he returned to the regular forms, retaining the play of contraries and deepening his view of the spirit of poetry: "Beyond the forms," he reiterated, "the poet is free. . . ."

Most important of all, the dark wanderer reflects, in the chiaroscuro setting of his choosing, on his own poetry as a forest of his own making, leaf to tree, leaf to page as in Neruda's meditation:

Libro	Book
hermoso,	beautiful,
libro	book
mínimo bosque.	minimal woods.

Desnos's theater of the text, which finally takes within itself the contemplation of the leaf, in its natural and literary sense, includes one of the "imperious themes" of "present inspiration" for which Desnos has such strong feeling. This, together with poetic technique, is the principal basis for his admiration for Góngora: "Villon, Gérard de Nerval, Góngora seem to me, with Baffo the Great, proper for contemporary reflections about poetic technique." Or again, from *Domaine public*:

> To unite popular language, the most popular, with an indescribable atmosphere and a sharp imagery; to annex domains which, even in our time, seem incompatible with the damned "noble language" which is ceaselessly born from the languages snatched from the mangy dog who protects the entrance of the poetic domain, that is what we need, but we must not forget, let me say it again, certain imperious themes of present inspiration. . . . (DP, 236)

Now, it should be noted that a French edition of *Las Soledades* of Góngora appeared in 1927, the very year of Desnos's *A la mystérieuse*; in both works, the major stress is on the lonely wandering of the poet through the text as if the journey were in fact interior to literature. This has already become clear in the comparison with Garcilaso, as the latter's words drying in the poet's mouth remind us of the leaves of Desnos's own hands and mouth, blocking his speech; these words and these leaves are the haunting images of a self-reflective poetry. For the forest ("selva") through which the poet Góngora wanders is at the same time the "silva" or forest of miscellaneous trees, and both these senses are inscribed in *Las Sole-*

dades, which is itself inscribed in a "silva." The famous lines beginning Góngora's sonnet to the Duke of Bejar give the reader his own path of correspondence, resonant with a paradoxical harmony.

> *Pasos de un peregrino son errantes*
> *cuantos me dicto versos dulce musa:*
> *en soledad confusa*
> *perdidos unos, otros inspirados.*

> A pilgrim's steps are wandering
> whatever poems did the sweet muse dictate to me:
> in loneliness confused
> Some are lost, others inspired.[8]

Here the following equation can be roughly established: soledad = selva = silva. That is to say, to write in a confused wood, or a *silva*, a stanzaless form, "a labyrinth of unequal lines and enmeshed rhythms—a metric forest, exuberant and undisciplined."[9] The form would then be exactly congruent with the idea of the poet's wandering transport; steps and verses are both lost and yet as if in Dante's "selva oscura," the Corsaire Sanglot wanders also in the baroque text.

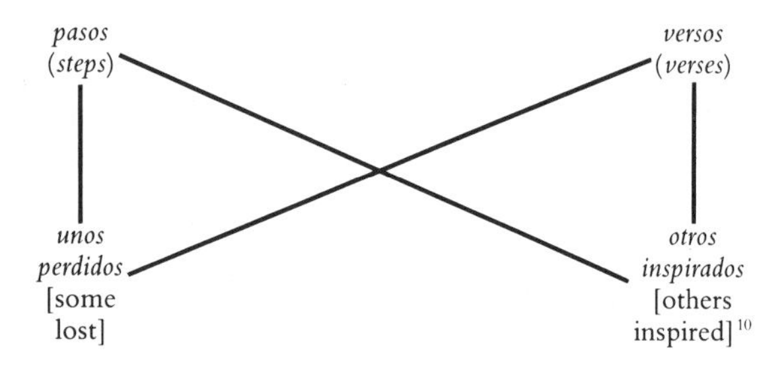

Góngora's solitude and Góngora's forest of words bring us closer to Desnos than had any previous poet, except Mallarmé. As the Corsaire Sanglot wanders through a world of his own making, his pilgrimage has the same self-referentiality as that of Scève and Desnos, and the same intense determination to preserve the passage in itself. In the late poetry of Desnos, the most striking verbs are those of arriving and departing and of motion through the field of poem, which is variously seen as cemetery, as harvest, as town, river, waterfall, and finally as the hill above the Country; this *Contrée*, sending us back to the *Eclogues* of Virgil, is found within the *Eglogas* of Garcilaso and retained as the ground for present poetry.

By one further parallelism, it might be seen that just these steps or *pasos . . . perdidos* are a prefiguration of the *pas perdus* of Breton, and are moreover inseparable from the *pasos inspirados*, all these lasting as long in the reader's mind as those steps whose uselessness Breton bemoans. Nadja, however, contradicts him: "*Lost Steps*? There are no lost steps," she claims, and I would echo that claim.

APOLLINAIRE AND HIS READERS

Crains qu'un jour un train ne t'émeuve plus.
Fear that some day a train may no longer move you.
GUILLAUME APOLLINAIRE, "La Victoire"

This two-way passage in time and text, placed as it is under the sign of "Le Voyageur" or the traveler, is dedicated to the memory of vision; the particular mental voyage will play back and forth between one and others, or the other incursions here, in an open correspondence and ambivalence, in a round trip endlessly remade.

As a starting point, we might consider two passages from Tristan Tzara in homage to Apollinaire. First, his moving poem on Apollinaire's death:

nous ne savons rien	we know nothing
nous ne savions rien de la douleur	we knew nothing of grief
. . .	. . .
ne pouvoir rien faire	to be unable to do anything[1]

And then Tzara wrote, twenty years after that lament and in an entirely different spirit, a text touched with sentimentality:

je pense à toi Guillaume carrefour
. . .
à travers toutes les pluies et les vents des pays
je retrouve le pavot de la mémoire

I think of you Guillaume crossroads
. . .
across all the rains and winds of countries
I find again the poppy of remembrance
(MC, 263)

Now any question of inheritance is likely to be a troubling one; to trouble the *source* in poetry is to risk disturbing the mystery to whose ambiguous shades the poem may owe its deepest debt. The knowledge gained, which some call "clarity" precisely for its triumph over the moving shadows, may prove a telling example of a game not quite worth its candle. Were it necessary to choose the background lighting for this set of cursory allusions to Apollinaire's legacy to the Dada and surrealist movements—taken here in the strongest sense of the word "movement," as the motion, for instance, of a voyage—it would most likely be that of the fiery principle of the candle as opposed to the electric light, despite Apollinaire's celebration of the "roses of electricity," which resembled the Italian futurist image of "electric moons." As justification, we need only notice the meteors gathered like bouquets of brilliant flowers in a city metamorphosed into a garden, and Apollinaire's multiple light-bearing images as they are linked to the figure of an all-devouring, violent, and self-willed flame, never to some temperate and controlled electric illumination fatal to mystery and shadow. For this perspective does not aim at the revelation of logic, but rather at the interior illumination of a possible road leading from more obvious influences and images to a flickering glimpse of some understated relations: "Cette flamme dont j'avais besoin, une bougie me la prêta, mobile comme le regard." ["This flame I needed, a candle lent it me, mobile like the gaze."][2] The quotation is from René Char, whose *Arsenal*, predating surrealism, already contains fire, even in its title (to burn: *ardre*), and whose arsenal of weapons outlasts periods and categories. "Je suis une flamme qui attend" ["I am a flame waiting"], says Apollinaire, to which Tzara replies later by the reversal of the image: "L'attente qui se fait flamme" ["The waiting become flame"].

"J'aime l'art aujourd'hui," says Apollinaire, "parce que j'aime avant tout la lumière et tous les hommes aiment avant tout la lumière, ils ont inventé le feu." ["I love today's art because I love light above everything else, and all men love light above everything else; they invented fire."][3] Apollinaire's burning temperament, extending to the universe in "La Jolie Rousse"—"O Soleil c'est le temps de la Raison ardente" ["O Sun, it's the time of ardent Reason"] causes heated passion to converge with tempered thought, in keeping with the oppositions and oxymorons of images and expressions inherent in the Dada and surrealist spirit and style, where the intense and privileged moment for the meeting of contraries is ardently illumined and repays meditation of its sublime point, like Breton's "point sublime."

Apollinaire's motto, "J'émerveille" ["I bring about wonder"] is appropriately linked to the surrealist marvelous, as, for instance, in the interpretation given by one critic[4] to three of the possible phonetic components of that expression: jet + mer + veille. The fountain ("jet") and the ocean ("mer") merge here with the nightwatcher's flame ("veille") so that, in a continuation of baroque imagery, water and fire may be seen to join in an implicit Bachelardian corridor, guided by the ardently selective finger of the candle. (I am thinking of such images as Georges de La Tour's famous *Madeleine à la veilleuse*, the subject of a poem by René Char, himself an heir to baroque imagery.[5])

Apollinaire's invocations to flame and fire include frequent allusions to the blazing vision of the poet whose eyes are themselves solar. In this respect, his poetry bears great similarities to the early poetry of Eluard, an example of which follows:

Je fis un feu, l'azur m'ayant abandonné
Un feu pour être son ami,
Un feu pour m'introduire dans la nuit d'hiver
Un feu pour vivre mieux.

I made a fire, the azure having left me
A fire to be its friend,
A fire to let me into winter's night
A fire to live better.[6]

One passage from Apollinaire's work—this one from "Le Brasier"—may represent all examples of his vision. In the poem, Apollinaire dedicates himself openly, as martyr and believer, to this unforgettable flame, which somehow absorbs the ocean at its source: again the contrary elements pass into one another like communicating vessels. A ritual baptism by flame and water is celebrated here:

Flamme je fais ce que tu veux

. . .

Qu'au brasier les flammes renaissent
Mon âme au soleil se dévêt

. . .

Je flambe dans le brasier à l'ardeur adorable
Et les mains des croyants m'y rejettent multiple innombrablement

. . .

Voici ma vie renouvelée
De grands vaisseaux passent et repassent
Je trempe une fois encore mes mains dans l'Océan
Voici le paquebot et ma vie renouvelée
Ses flammes sont immenses
Il n'y a plus rien de commun entre moi
Et ceux qui craignent les brûlures

Flame I do your bidding

. . .

Let the flames be reborn in the live-coal fire
My soul strips in the sun

. . .

I flame in the fire's adorable ardor
And the believers' hands cast me back there multiple innumerably

. . .

Here is my life renewed
Great vessels pass and pass by again
I dip once more my hands into the Ocean
Here is the steamer and my life renewed
Its flames are immense

I have nothing in common
With those who fear burnings[7]

The steamers or those other vessels, in their own right, pass by still in surrealism, for Desnos will see them also, and everywhere, elements in his own ritual of passage just as surely as the dipping of hands in water. Kindred spirits such as Tzara's Approximate Man awaiting the flame in his desert, or Breton's narrator in "Vigilance," setting his own bed afire to approach the center of things in yet another rite of passage, or then Aragon's active poet, surround the poet dancing amid the fire of eyes in Aragon's collection of 1919 called *Feu de joie* [*Bonfire*]:

Je danse au milieu des miracles
Mille soleils peints sur le sol
Mille amis Mille yeux ou monocles
M'illuminent de leurs regards
. . .
Je saute ainsi d'un jour à l'autre
. . .
Je brûlerai du feu des phares

I dance in the middle of miracles
A thousand suns painted on the ground
A thousand friends A thousand eyes or monocles
Illuminate me with their gazes
. . .
Thus I skip by from one day to the next
. . .
I shall burn with lighthouse fire[8]

Potentially linking the act of writing with that of living, the hand vitalizes, threatens, and is the privileged agent of *ardor*. The innumerable hands casting the body of the poet and of poetry into the brazier's flame, as Apollinaire sees it, cause the image to flicker and to live: The renewed life is literally renovated in its form, in so many pulsations: "Voici ma vie renouvelée . . . Voici le paquebot et ma vie renouvelée." With the revivification of vision comes the ever-wider multiplication of possibilities of act, and of spheres of action of which Apollinaire makes himself the fervent singer: "Je chante toutes les possibilités de moi-même hors de ce monde et des astres" ["I sing all the possibilities of myself outside this world and stars"].

As for the gathering of possibilities, Apollinaire successfully assembles fragmented conversations into speech, the promises held out by posters and prospectuses, into such reality as the poem has ("Il y a . . . Il y a . . ." ["There is . . . There is . . ."]), and makes of his enthusiastic wandering a contemporary version of the traditional quest. When, in his turn, Breton transmutes Apollinaire's vivid enumeration or catalog and Eluard's corresponding caution, ("Il y aurait un homme . . . sinon il n'y aurait rien" ["There would be a man . . . If not, there would be nothing"]) (OC, I, 1108), into a summons to the marvelous, "Il y aura une fois" ["Once upon a time there will be"], he alters the fairy tale formula, "Once upon a time there was," in the sense of the surrealist's meliorative vision. The latter is well illustrated in the anecdote Breton recounts of the Zen master Bashô correcting his disciple who, seeing a dragonfly with its wings removed as a red pepper, corrected him to say that one should add wings to a red pimento to make it a dragonfly. *There will be*, then, what the multiple vision will choose to imagine as real. The marvelous, we remember, tends to become the actual. That is still the motto for the wandering of "Le Voyageur" as reader, who detects actual signals along the streets of Apollinaire's Paris, where they beckon from the walls, like "so many white signs" or emerge as street cries of poetic "errance" (the original title of "Zone" was in fact "Cri," a shrill signal indeed).

But poetry is made as much by the mouth as by the eye: For Apollinaire, consonants signifying nothing other than their sound, tappings on the cheek, burps and loud expectorations, all these are its *stuff*. The linguistic experiments of Desnos's *Langage cuit* and *P'Oasis*, or of Aragon's *Le Mouvement perpétuel*, of Breton's *Le Corset mystère*, call on slightly differing rules, and the name of the game may differ; nevertheless, the serious and liberating intent implied in the game is unmistakably similar. Thus, the general attitude to scene and sound provides a propitious field for the continued and acknowledged inheritance of an ardent and paradoxical reason, its flame commanding a commanding voice, from Apollinaire's "voix qui clame," not in a desert but a city, to the surrealist summons made by "The Voice of Robert Desnos": "J'appelle à moi . . . J'appelle à moi . . ." ["I call to myself . . . I call to myself"].[9]

And poetry calls upon the hand. That a poet should be haunted by the image of a writing hand or a hand pointing, or trembling, or even wounded, may seem only poetic justice. For the hand is first of all the agent of the literary order of language; an assault upon it is an assault upon action and poetic creation itself. Apollinaire sees a hand "suddenly placed" before his eyes, disorienting the sight, similar to Eluard's vision in one of his gloomiest poems, "Défense de savoir":

Née de la main sur mes yeux	Born of my hand over my eyes
Et me détournant de ma voie	And turning me aside from my path
L'ombre m'empêche de marcher	The shadow keeps me from walking
Sur ma couronne d'univers . . .	On the crown of my universe . . . (FOC, 215)

And in Apollinaire's "Palais," a pair of hands is placed against a windowpane and stigmatized with blood; elsewhere they are shaking like a leaf and still again are seen severed from the body. The attention is focused on wounding and malady, on hesitation and separation, quite as horribly as in the long passage from Desnos's *Night of Loveless Nights*, from which even a few lines give the tone:

> *Il y a les mains terribles*
> *Main noircie d'encre de l'écolier triste*
> *Main rouge sur le mur de la chambre du crime*
> *Main pâle de la morte*
>
> . . .

Mains abjectes qui tiennent un porte-plume
O ma main toi aussi toi aussi
Ma main avec tes lignes et pourtant c'est ainsi

There are the terrible hands
Ink-blackened hand of the sad schoolboy
Red hand on the wall of the room of crime
Pale hand of the dead woman

. . .

Abject hands grasping a penholder
Oh my hand you too you too
My hand with your lines and still that's the way it is

(DP, 231)

In these cases, the imagery seems to mock the writing hand, and thus of the poet's own creating, as if the mechanism of production might have gone awry under the pressure of once-automatic or semiautomatic experimentation, cutting off irreparably the agent from the willing mind as a ghastly punishment for having meddled with the traditional inscription of the word. Apollinaire's extraordinary text called simply "Table" is a meditation upon the conditions of writing: the table's shape, the pen and ink, the lighting, the position of the writer; it makes an art of nearsightedness. In similar fashion, the narrator of Desnos's great novel *La Liberté ou l'amour!* concentrates upon his own ink and pen, upon writing, its instruments, and its effect on the number of times he writes a word like "love." "Banality! Banality!," he cries, keeping his distance: "The one I love: I've not told you her name. . . ." Both poets, akin in many of their motifs and themes as in their changing tones and rhythms, are obsessed by the image of the writing hand, like tragic ancestors of the lighter spirit of Saul Steinberg's cartoons and Le Clézio's concentration on his own *écriture*.

"Je suis ganté" ["I am gloved"]; this line from Apollinaire's highly charged prose poem *Oneirocritique* (OP, 373) could be read as a suppression of the image of hands, for they are first seen pointing like steeples, then as flames, and finally as losing their unique power of designation when they are thus sheathed. And yet of course a covered image is potentially revealed, is latent and omnipresent like the surrealist gods. It is, in fact, singled out, as is the face wearing a mask: when the glove is turned inside out, a vague anguish is produced: all of these signals are illustrated in Giorgio de Chirico's early canvasses. Red gloves, empty gloves, gloves on a chess board or hanging inert, pinned upon a wall.

The same pull explicit in the rhythmic build-up and letdown, and left implicit between the hand writing and the hand mocked is established between Apollinaire's ardent will to motion, "Allons plus vite" ["Let's go more quickly"], and his mockery concluding with the tragic realization of the limits of that motion, rapid or not, "Toujours nous irons plus loin sans avancer jamais" ["Always we'll go further without ever moving forward" OP, 237]. Most notably, Apollinaire's play *Couleur du temps* [*Color of Time*] of 1918, with its deserted island at the South Pole as the fatal end of a voyage and the ice floes in one of which a woman's body is buried, another mockery of the ideal, bears a resemblance to André Gide's *Voyage d'Urien* [*Voyage of Nothing*] and then finds an inheritor in Desnos's *La Liberté ou l'amour!* of 1928 with its venturing ship stuck in the polar ice floes, its hero stranded in the desert, its skeletons of mermaids and cadavers of beautiful swimmers representing the unfortunate end of adventure, and thus the end of the lyric temptation to any possible further voyage. The play of white images in Apollinaire leads on, from Milky Way and sea foam to an icy Mallarméan lake where a few swans make a phonetic mirror or *glace* for the white signs, those *cygnes/signes.* The signals once again ("combien de signes blancs") attract the voyaging gaze.

Voie lactée ô soeur lumineuse
Des blancs ruisseaux de Chanaan
Et des corps blancs des amoureuses
Nageurs morts suivrons-nous d'ahan
Ton cours vers d'autres nébuleuses

. . .

Près d'un château sans châtelaine

La barque aux barcarols chantants
Sur un lac blanc et sous l'haleine
Des vents qui tremblent au printemps
Voguait cygne mourant sirène

Milky way, oh luminous sister
Of Canaan's white streams
And of the lovers' white bodies
Dead swimmers we will strive to follow
The course you take toward other nebulae

. . .

Near a castle with no chatelaine
The ship with singing barcaroles
On a white lake and under the breath
Of the winds trembling in spring
A swan drifted dying mermaid

"La Chanson du mal-aimé" (OP, 58)

Apollinaire's signals mark the way forward to Tzara's white passages in *L'Homme approximatif* of 1920 to 1925, "Dehors tout est blanc" ["Outside all is white"], as well as to Desnos's parody of it all, a shellac lake where a few peacocks are stuck, like remnants of the symbolist menagerie or bestiary, "Aux lacs des lacs / meurent les paons / enlisés dans la gomme laque" ["In the lakes of lakes / the peacocks die / Stuck in the shellac"] (DP, 66).

The memorable chapter of ill-fated wandering entitled "The Bay of Hunger" in the long poetic novel Desnos called, in a perfect ambivalence, *Freedom or Love!* lead to the epic battles fought with swords and star beams in his long poem of 1930 that bears only an English title: *The Night of Loveless Nights.* These wanderings and these battles waged between the mermaid and her luminous sisters the stars at midnight in the Milky Way recall, in tone, rhythm, and figures, Apollinaire's own *Oneirocritique.* That most remarkable text is informed by a multiplying vision equalled only by that of Eluard's expansive and expanding consciousness and is mirrored on the linguistic side by Artaud's frenzied prose poems such as *L'En-*

clume des forces and by Desnos's experiments in linguistic and imaged transformations.

In *Oneirocritique*, "le chant des champs" ["the song of the fields"] yields a litanic structure and an almost hieratic scene, where the coals of the sky are on the point of burning the narrator, where rivers are changed to swords as they are brandished, where teeth change to snakes and to tongues, where pirates and golden vessels without sailors are depicted against a canvas of epic scope, most akin to those of Desnos's *Deuil pour deuil* and *Siramour*, the latter filled with mermaids, pirates, and oceans, skies and stars, castles, and corridors. Little wonder that Apollinaire's narrator and his vision are both increased a hundred times, thus increasing the reader's own. It is worth noting that, as Eluard and Breton often do, Apollinaire situates his text in the initial framework of near burning; it is thus, like so many of theirs, an ardent text, an *arsenal* at its inception, a passage marked by a flaming threshold:

> *Les charbons du ciel étaient si proches que je craignais leur ardeur. Ils étaient sur le point de me brûler. Mais j'avais la conscience des éternités différentes de . . . l'homme et de la femme.*
>
> *A quatre pattes, à quatre pattes.*
>
> *Mes bras, mes jambes se ressemblaient et mes yeux multipliés me couronnaient attentivement. Je me relevais ensuite et pour danser comme les mains et les feuilles.*
>
> . . .
>
> *Je me désespérai. Mais, j'avais la conscience des éternités différentes de . . . l'homme et de la femme. Des ombres dissemblables assombrissaient de leur amour l'écarlate des voilures, tandis que mes yeux se multipliaient dans les fleuves, dans les villes et sur la neige des montagnes.*

The coals of the sky were so near I feared their heat. They were about to burn me. But I was conscious of the different eternities of . . . man and woman.

. . .

On all fours, on all fours.

My arms, my legs resembled each other and my multiplied eyes crowned me attentively. I picked myself up then to dance like hands and leaves.

. . .

I despaired. But I was conscious of the different eternities of . . . man and woman. Dissimilar shadows darkened with their love the veiling scarlet, while my eyes were multiplied in the rivers, the towns, and upon the snow of mountains. (OP, 374)

The most effective of Eluard's prose poems are based on just such repetitions and lyric suspensions ["Mais j'avais . . . Mais j'avais"], and Desnos's novels find their high points in this kind of incantation; the play of halt against forward movement, of repetition against expansion, is as haunting on the formal plane as the images of motion and motion arrested to which the style so perfectly corresponds.

As for the motion apparently arrested or mocked as in *Couleur du temps*, its most celebrated surrealist representation is no doubt Breton's train in *Nadja* always about to leave the Gare de Lyon, shaking with the convulsive beauty of action played against fixity, that train of which Breton says, "Je sais qu'il ne va jamais partir, qu'il n'est pas parti." ["I know it will never depart, has not departed"].[10] Beauty, thus made of fits and starts, is destined to bring one day a great convulsion of epic reach. The clash between opposed elements, the violence of a departure endlessly halted, convulses the image whose intensity inspires the text, as in the surrealist train hurtling at top speed but halted in a virgin forest, and parallels the line, which like surrealist love, begins "Toujours pour la première fois" ["Always for the first time"]. These images seem themselves the extension of a sublime point at which extremes meet without reduction; they find their common ancestor in Apollinaire's own sublimity of contraries, a product of his ardent reason.

As writing and motion are mocked, and somehow celebrated in that mocking, so too are vision and language. Even Breton's window in *Arcane 17* is overgrown with ivy, as if sight itself were to be blocked, thwarted in its traverse; and yet, to be sure, mystery and the marvelous are thus preserved. It is natural for the idea of vision to have an outward and inward component; the outward or formal component is partially illustrated or framed by windows and their opening, by the roundness of the blazing sun and ripe fruit in clear colors, stressing the intensity of the seeing eye and the fullness of its wide-ranging gaze, linked, as we have seen, to the clarity and freshness of morning. On the other side, the myth of vision is frequently undone from inside and out, in the rhythm now familiar to us, both from Apollinaire's texts such as "Les Fenêtres" and in those of the great surrealist poets. Robert Desnos, a great master of language and vision built up and then destroyed, undoes the text and its language in multiple ways. After a long and subtle discourse, he exclaims naively: "Qu'ai-je dit?/Je n'ai rien dit." ["What did I say?/I said nothing"].[11]

Similarly, in Apollinaire's work, a mocking laughter or then an acknowledgment of bitter deception follows often hard upon passages of sight and clarity. In "La Victoire," ironically for a poem on victory and exhilarated discourse, two lamps burning may be seen as two women laughing: "Je courbe tristement la tête / Devant l'ardente moquerie/Ce rire se répand/Partout" ["I bend my head sadly/ Before the ardent mockery / This laughter spreads / Everywhere"] (OP. 311). Such ardent mockery[12] is reproduced by the convergence of exterior light and interior obsession; self-inflicted, it can contaminate all vision and all surroundings. This poem begins with a false Icarus and will end in linguistic triumph. Yet here at the center there is at least a partial defeat, resounding in the same way that certain passages of Desnos resound, unforgettably.

In many cases, the fatal form of construction and then of destruction sets a limit on the thing perceived: the train speeding by ("Crains qu'un jour un train ne t'émeuve / Plus" ["Fear that some day a train may no longer / Move you"]) is rapidly followed by its reduction, the warning that the railroad tracks, beautiful and useless, may lead straight out of real life. In particular, intensity and ardor are destined to grow cold and the epiphanic consciousness turns sour even in its most apparently available form, a deliberate fixation on one image as a condensation of ennobling vision. Even the red hair of "La Jolie Rousse" ["The Pretty Redhead"] of 1918, compared first to a lasting lightning flash and then to flames, even this burning vision is challenged by a deception, for the flame is found in a tea-rose color rapidly fading. And once again, in this "time of ardent reason," the narrator first seeks pity and then finally accepts the mockery he seems to claim for and inflict upon himself at his lack of speech.

Mais riez riez de moi
Car il y a tant de choses que je n'ose vous dire
Tant de choses que vous ne me laisseriez pas dire
Ayez pitié de moi

But laugh laugh at me
For there are so many things I dare not say to you
So many things you wouldn't let me say
Take pity on me (OP, 314)

Again, Desnos furnishes the closest interior parallel. At the end of each poetic adventure, especially in *Les Ténèbres* of 1927 and in *La Liberté ou l'amour!* of 1928, after each ascent of the mountain and the return, after the dream and the quest, the edelweiss gathered on the highest peak is seen to wither, the flowers to fade, the voyaging vessel is stranded in ice floes or in the desert, and the vision does not even outlast its transcription, becoming only dry leaves in the mouth, which then denies the speech that issued from it ("What did I say? Nothing"). Despite the presumed power of poetic language, the person called upon does not answer, while all the glorious images of the symbolist era are shifted toward the tragic:

Les ongles des femmes seront des cygnes étranglés
Pas très loin d'ici une herbe sèche sur le bord du chemin

The women's nails will be strangled swans
Not far away a herb dries on the edge of the path.
(DP, 139)[13]

Compare these lines from Desnos to those of Apollinaire's "Mai" from his Rhenish poems:

Or des vergers fleuris se figeaient en arrière
Les petales tombées des cerisiers de mai
Sont les ongles de celle que j'ai tant aimée
Les pétales flétries sont comme ses paupières

Now flowered orchards grew rigid afterwards
The fallen petals of May's cherry trees
Are the nails of the one I so loved
The withered petals are like her eyelids.

(OP, 111)

But despite such deception, poisoning in advance all images and creation and self-reflective vision, a certain hope, similar in the works of the two poets, remains for language. As Apollinaire's pretty redhead teaches us, the finest victories are often those won against finitude and limited by an ardor that corresponds to Breton's "état d'attente." They are won textually also against language itself, by a call to laughter or by a fearful silence, where the unspoken gives its intensity to the unfinished. Apollinaire's "Victory" claims a noble quest, where the open-mouthed "O" precedes the statement "l'homme est . . .": "O bouches l'homme est à la recherche d'un nouveau langage" ["O mouths man seeks a new language"]. When "La Jolie rousse" invokes a "bouche qui est l'ordre même" ["mouth which is order itself"] (OP, 313), it is as if the mouth of poetry in its universal appetite and thirst were finally to be the source of a new order of song, as in Apollinaire's "Vendémiaire," which is only matched in ardor by Desnos's own fervent intoxication apparent in the early works. Apollinaire, exalted, speaks loudly:

Je suis ivre d'avoir bu tout l'univers

. . .

Ecoutez-moi je suis le gosier de Paris
Et je boirai encore s'il me plaît l'univers
Ecoutez mes chants d'universelle ivrognerie

I am tipsy from having drunk the whole universe

. . .

Listen to me I'm the throat of Paris
And I'll drink the universe if I wish to
Listen to my songs of universal intoxication

(OP, 154)

And on the September night drawing slowly to an end, the red bridge lights fade like the stars, and the day is reborn, baptized, after the drunken night of passage. The source of song is once more located at the point of dawn, and a passionate conviction endures past the weakening light of the stars into what is about to be: "il y aura. . . ." At daybreak renewed, when Apollinaire's cock crow in "La Victoire" announces his dream and that of Desnos, if the reader so chooses, the ardor of language suffices in this splendid song of triumph through mockery.

New things are seen and heard in all their joyousness in Apollinaire's victory song of poetry, and renewed readings bear witness to "ignorance" and "errance" as inspirations for the voice of the truest traveler:

O voix je parle le langage de la mer

. . .

La rue où nagent mes deux mains
Aux doigts subtils fouillant la ville
S'en va mais qui sait si demain
La rue devenait immobile
Qui sait où serait mon chemin

Oh voice, I speak the language of the sea

. . .

The street where my two hands swim,
Their subtle fingers exploring the town,
Goes its way, but who knows
If the street became immobile tomorrow
Who knows where my path would lead

(OP, 311)

In another sort of liquid song, issuing from a "Rhenish Night" ("Nuit rhénane"), the wine bubbling in a glass leads to a boatman's slow song, a dance with girls near the drunken Rhine, and then to a burst of literally shattering laughter as the expression "rire aux éclats" is matched by shards of glass. The wine will again tremble in the poetry of Desnos, as will the laughter, ardent as the other "flaming" liquid shattering the surface of the poem:

> *Mon verre est plein d'un vin trembleur comme une flamme*
>
> . . .
>
> *Mon verre s'est brisé comme un éclat de rire*
>
> My glass is full of a wine quavering like a flame
>
> . . .
>
> My glass has shattered like a burst of laughter
>
> (OP, 111)

Again enthusiasm leads to explicit breakage and implicit mockery, in the now familiar rhythm of construction and deconstruction on which the novels and many of the great poems of Desnos, as well as of Apollinaire, are based. Myths are elaborated and exposed, repetitions built up to intensity and then truncated, stage sets erected at length and taken for real, then accused of being only stage sets, visions enlarged and intensified, then mocked; but that mocking laughter, like the drunkenness, forms a major part of the poetry.

But finally, the real victory, that of all poets, is also that of the reader, to whose own self-definition the poem makes its urgent appeal for nomination as for ardent vision. The reader is called upon to see, beyond the simple catalogs of enumeration, to the hopeful expression "there is," and to a list of all that is around to be pointed out, and then to the "once upon a time there will be" with its rapid and vitalizing shift from far to near:

Regarde	Look
La Victoire avant tout sera	Victory will be above all
De bien voir au loin	To see far into the distance
De tout voir	To see everything
De près	Close up
Et que tout ait un nom nouveau	And for everything to have a new name (OP, 312)

In the long run it matters little what that new name is, or from what vocabulary the description of an also historical victory is taken: cubism, orphism, simultanism, futurism, Dada, surrealism. Art does not change, as Apollinaire is supposed to have remarked to Breton (PC, 24).

In the cortege of movements and notions, literary or human, each of us might be seen from far off as sometimes drab or even slow in perception, as somber, improperly suited to intoxication, uncomprehending of the potential clash of contraries radiant and quivering within a sublime point or trembling within an ardent liquid; in short, we might seem to be of a dull approach. We might, however, seem somehow different close up, situated in what there now is and yet luminous in what we pass toward, in a once-upon-a-time that may finally be:

> *Et moi aussi de près je suis sombre et terne*
>
> . . .
>
> *Et je m'éloignerai m'illuminant . . .*
>
> And I too close up I am somber and dull
>
> . . .
>
> And I shall pass into the distance lighting up . . .
>
> (OP, 74)

Once upon a time then, in that far off point of ardent convergence, those who fear no burning—to use an expression of Apollinaire, and not the least moving of them—may perceive the convulsive correspondence or the radiant passage obtaining between a luminous distance: "Et je m'éloignerai m'illuminant," and a present vision: "Je brûle parmi vous" ["I burn among you"], as absence and presence find their equal and victorious illumination.

III. METAPOETIC MODERNS

The four poets chosen in this final self-reflective passage represent four different ways of turning about the central theme and the literary consciousness it entails; together they range over a wide scope of contemporary poetry and poetics. Char's firm espousal of a path for poetry at once private and cosmic sets up a vibration between contrasts of brightest clarity and blackest dark, between fire and snow, like the contemporary equivalent of the consciously passionate surrealist play of opposites. Garelli's studies of the rhythmic alternation from the moment of rupture to the moment of completion, from stress to silence, from explosion to dispersion, and from paradox to paradox exemplify what they examine, the temporal pulse of a living poetry. Deguy's insistence on the specific place where one thing or concept passes to the next, on the hinge or link of a threshold sensibility, is spatial rather than temporal. Situated *between*, he is inclined toward the notion of twinnings, toward the accomplishment of two actions at once and the reflexive play of their juxtaposition. Dupin's texts lead up and down, from mounting to crumbling: "Gravir" to "Eboulement," or then in and out, from inscription to extension, from an interior trace to the one sketched outside.

The configuration of these four essays repeats in microcosm the outline initially sketched for this volume: a general discussion of the rupture and gaps within the text seen as a speech event constantly examining its own passage, as a spatially and temporally mobile self-creation, corresponding to the breach of the former poetic code.

From the enabling ground of the metaphors and the detailed images with which it is connected, out to its wider situation and development, the way taken by these essays may be seen to engage in a self-reflection and a self-reflexion. It makes no attempt at completion, for if a book concerning passage were to arrest a free flow of works by a limiting statement, the passage itself would be but a freeze frame. I might say of these final essays what Dupin says of the narrator who may turn out after all to be the poet:

Il m'est interdit de m'arrêter pour voir. Comme si j'étais condamné à voir en marchant.

> I was forbidden to stop in order to see. As if I were condemned to see while walking. (EM, 139)

Only by a sufficient stress on mobility may critical perception hope to avoid the perils of static fixation, even a fixation on what is evolving.

RENÉ CHAR
Path and Passerby

Qui délivrera le message n'aura pas d'identité. Il n'oppressera pas.
The one delivering the message will have no identity. He will not oppress.
RENÉ CHAR, *Aromates chasseurs*[1]

INTERROGATION

Great poetry is its own examination, as we know, posing its own problems to which it already supplies the richest response. And insofar as it answers, it interrogates the reader in turn: "The interrogative response is the response of being" (AC, 18). For example, Char's "Réviseur" and his "Etoile de mer" take up earlier texts, condensing their accumulated energy in expression and in thought and rethinking them for an even sharper intensity of focus. They are meant to serve as examples of the poet's own passage through his poems, in their making.[2]

So as not to reduce the density of the two statements, I will treat them here one after the other, to finally superimpose them one upon the other. A universe is constant in each poem, as we have been taught by Char himself over the years, each poem sufficing unto itself to say the whole. It is as if each new text were now to bring us, in its retrospective wake, others too numerous to mention, so that ramifications abound.

LE RÉVISEUR

Il m'était difficile de faire glisser mon imagination au milieu de tant de calme. A l'entrée même de ce mot creux où rien de ce qui nous élève ne retentit plus. C'était si bas, si bas devant mes pieds et sans une trace d'air. . . . Je parviendrai à m'y étendre. Mais seule la poésie, au sortir des misères et des splendeurs de la vie, la courtisane au collier de fer, devait permettre l'accolade véridique, et peut-être consentirait-elle à me la donner pour autant que je ne l'aie point déçue, si inapte suis-je à me retourner. Je ne lui demandais que le viatique vicariant, pas davantage. De frénétiques délateurs, des bourreaux tranquilles, à l'ouvrage dans l'univers, s'appliquaient selon des préceptes supérieurs. Sur l'écran de ma veille, face à la glace diffusante des lunes et des soleils, le monde quotidien de l'internement, de la filature, de la déportation, des supplices et de la crémation devenait pyramidal à l'image du haut négoce qui prospérait sous sa potence en or. Mais j'avais vu grandir, écarlate, l'arrière-fleur aux doigts du ferronnier, bondir de son berceau l'eau dédiée à la nuit. Comme un lac de montagne avoisinant la neige et le hameau, j'avais vécu.

THE EXAMINER

It was hard for me to insert my imagination into the center of such calm. At the very entrance of this hollow word where nothing that uplifts us resounds any longer. So very low it was, low before my feet and without a trace of air. . . . I shall manage to stretch out there. But poetry alone, at the outcome of life's miseries and splendors, the iron-collared courtisan, could permit the embrace of truth, and would perhaps consent to grant it to me, since I have in no way deceived her, inept as I am at turning. I asked from her only the vicarious viaticum, no more. Frenzied informers, tranquil executioners, active throughout the universe, busied themselves according to loftier precepts. On the screen of my watchfulness, confronting the diffusing mirror of moons and suns, the daily world of internments, of tracking, of deportation, of torture and cremation, took the form of a pyramid reflecting the business which prospered under its golden gibbet. But I had seen the late flower growing, scarlet, in the ironmonger's fingers, seen the night-pledged water bounding from its cradle. As a mountain lake, neighbor to snow and hamlet, I had lived my life.[3]

"The Examiner" seems, in fact, to examine a lifetime: to commence with the difficulty of imagining nonbeing, its calm and silence, the airlessness of the narrow space remembered from one of the poems in "Abondance viendra" (*Le Marteau sans maître* [*The Hammer with No Master*]). This low-lying room sets up an extraordinary resonance with the burial in "Devancier" ["Forerunner"] from *Le Nu perdu* [*Bareness Lost*] with its bedrock rising to a grave chiseled out in the air, befitting the poet's return to the sky. Even there the *extension* is required as it is within this text, and not just that of the poet's figurative body ("Je parviendrai à m'y étendre" ["I shall manage to stretch out there,"] RC, 204–5). No other companion to embrace, at the moment of crisis and limit, but poetry; herein one is faithful always to the uncompromising and the "insoumis," like this brutal brother whom Char himself has always been, "ce compère indélébile que nous sommes quelques-uns à avoir fréquenté" (["this indelible companion whose friendship some of us have kept,"] RC, 53–54). Even though this poem predicts the poet's eventual departure, he stakes out intensely his moral claim on our lasting affection and our uncompromising judgment. An inviolable claim: from it the reader might learn not to turn about, not to double back and compromise, to strike no easy bargains. And yet, "Il n'y a pas de siège pur" ["There is no untainted seat,"] we learned in "J'habite une douleur" (["A Pain I Dwell In,"] RC, 104–5). Is a compromise then necessary in that dwelling?

The sleep of the narrator in this last poem, like the sleep of that other "extreme" narrator in "L'Extravagant" (RC, 108–9) is as light as the dream "of the morrow." A few white birds pass across the ceiling, reminding us of the village of birds passing high above in the poem "Conduite" ["Convey"], which precedes the epic love poem called "Le Visage nuptial," conveying its vision onward, and then to the countenance of the reader also, whose look is wedded to that of the poet, from now on. The aromatic colors of a lunar landscape direct the reader's thoughts now toward the later volume of *Aromates chasseurs*, for the net of all these poems has itself become a landscape, sufficient for dwelling. But whether the birds pass high above, or across the ceiling, their *passage* too, like that of the reader, is inextricably interwoven with the text as it becomes one with the "screen of my watchfulness" or its equivalent, "the diffusing mirror. . . ." The self-contemplating narrator, whose speaking voice retains a mysterious edge to it, is never himself tempted to soar in imitation: "We feel completely detached from Icarus who willed himself a bird" (RC, 199). He is rather one who has rendered his unique service and must now take his leave. The dignity and calm of the description contrasts with the frenzied scurrying about of the informers and the executioners, recalling the note to a friend, the "Billet à Francis Curel" written after the war, in its description of a handful of little beasts demanding the slaughter of a prey they had not themselves even hunted (RBS, 16).[4] Char refuses both imitation and vicarious condemnation, just as he scorns the necessity of compromise and the unthinking and often self-serving business of the crowd. A poem at least partly political comes to mind, "Mirage des aiguilles" ["Mirage of the Peaks"] found—and not by accident—in the same volume as the text of Icarus refused. In the poem, things are subtle beyond the reach of a simplistic political left or right:

Ils prennent pour de la clarté le rire jaune des ténèbres. Ils soupèsent dans leurs mains les restes de la mort et s'écrient: 'Ce n'est pas pour nous.' Aucun viatique précieux n'embellit la gueule de leurs serpents déroulés.

They take for clarity the jaundiced laughter of shadows. They weigh in their hands death's remains and exclaim: 'This is not for us.' No precious viaticum embellishes the mouth of their uncoiled snakes. (RC, 202–3)

Be warned, the narrator of the mirage continues, and so should we be.

The world of espionage and daily business has neither reflective power nor emotion, neither irony nor principles, and thus incites Char's utter scorn. In another land, behind this one, an "arrière-fleur" grows scarlet, the color of the absent brother's audacity first perceived so long ago and yet remaining so constant. The water is refreshed there, and from its very distance it draws the power to heal the imagination the scurrying world would trivialize, and to restore it: "Boire frileusement, être brutal répare." ["To drink shivering, to be brutal restores you," RC, 254–55]. The red of this flower serves as complement to the blue of the flower Apollon gathers and then crushes, with his clumsy tenderness, in *Le Soleil des eaux* [*The Sun of Waters*]. Here in "Le Réviseur" the distance is kept: the flower grows, but grows apart from the narrator's vision. Like the corresponding image of the "night-pledged water" in its traditional setting, for a symbol of renewing, it is the fragile bearer of a future hope. The conclusion of this poem is itself refreshed or restored by the mountain lake, as is the concluding line of "L'Amoureuse en secret" ["Loving in Secret," RC, 126–27] where a bed trembles in exile, "comme un lac de montagne qui ne sera jamais abandonné" ["like a mountain lake never to be abandoned"]. The text ends in its own summary statement of an ending: "J'avais vécu," which acts as culmination but not as closure.

Thus the poem moves from the initial prediction of death toward the final completion and contemplation of life. It is stretched between this entrance turning about an exit and this exit turning about a lifetime, seen from what is a passionately involved point of view, wonderfully illogical: "I had lived my life."

Such a poem sums up a life imbuing us with a moral passion, measuring all acts and all vision. It is then the opposite of a coffin in which to stretch out, the opposite, too, of a low and confined space. Char's attitude, often qualified as "heroic," translates here into a slightly different tone from that which we sense in his resistance poems: it too has grown and has, in a certain sense, grown more scarlet, like that flower flourishing in his back country. His resistance poetry, splendid in its fury and yet its intense mystery—*Fureur et mystère* (1938–1947)—combined then as always in Char's work—had not then attained the depth sensible here. It took, perhaps, the passage by another kind of suffering, the furrow traced in the mind and heart not just by the imagination of death (that "Fleur traversée d'un secret continu" ["Flower valleyed by a steady secret"], RC, 200–1), but by the profound difficulties in love and living that leave traces of bodily and mental grief: the title "J'habite une douleur" speaks for itself. Now, to follow the image in that poem's title, all the rooms have been inhabited.

Elsewhere I have tried to point out the gradual deepening of the water images and their significance in this poetry, tried to trace the patterns we recognize variously in fountain, spring, river, and—less often—sea, starting with a mere glass of water carried by Artine in 1930 and moving to the source most gravely traced: this passage seeming the gravest. The path followed "amont," upland toward the summit of a mountain or upstream toward the springing of a water, is that difficult traverse along which the poems are themselves arranged, and is thus the path the reader too must follow. At this point in Char's passage, this water is fully dedicated to the night: "L'eau dédiée à la nuit."

In *La Nuit talismanique* [*Talismanic Night*] of 1972, there was already flowing the water of dream, which inspired the surrealist imaginings long before, and Char's own, in *Artine* and in "Abondance viendra." One has only to re-read some of the poems in *Le Marteau sans maître* to find that source. But the breadth and depth of this poetry is now other. "As everyone knows, meditation and water are wedded forever," we read in *Moby Dick*,[5] and we are summoned back by many of Char's comments to the tone of Melville, one of his great "alliés substantiels" and privileged predecessors:

Je me suis uni au courage de quelques êtres, j'ai vécu violemment, sans vieillir, mon mystère au milieu d'eux, j'ai frissonné de l'existence de tous les autres, comme une barque incontinente au-dessus des fonds cloisonnés.

I have joined in the courage of a few beings, have lived violently, without growing older, my mystery in their midst, I have trembled at the existence of all the others like an incontinent boat above the partitioned depths. (RC, 212–13)

"J'ai vécu . . . j'ai frissonné": the statement will never be more personal than that, or more collective in its "partage commun." As we re-read *Redburn*, *Billy Budd*, *Moby Dick*, *White Jacket*, we find this text again, in its essential image of a passage above the water with one's companions, found and then, chosen. In particular, the image of a lofty vantage point will recur, and no one has described better than Char's Melville (for through his eyes we see the American afresh) the spirit of the "airy perch" in its loneliness and its unique companionship. "We maintop men were brothers, one and all; and we loaned ourselves to each other with all the freedom in the world" (WJ, 27). Or again, seen from the narrator's point of view, similar to that of the airy perch, but to whose expression the third-person form lends a different tone: ". . . the reason of their lofty-mindedness was that they were high lifted above the petty tumults, carping cares, and paltrinesses of the decks below" (WJ, 57). The attitude is raised above compromise as above ease.

Now if that tone and attitude are joined with the unforgiving struggle toward a summit or a mountain peak, as in the *Recherche de la base et du sommet* [*Search for the Base and the Summit*] or *Retour amont* [*Return Upland*], the landscape merges with a seascape as in the magnificent and yet quiet poem, "Fastes" ["Annals," RC, 84–85], where the peaks of foam can suddenly be seen to form a mountain setting, even in the sea.[6] Melville's *Pierre, or the Ambiguities*, to whose own ironic depiction of life some of Char's work is closely related, is dedicated to a mountain—and, specifically, to one of Vermont's White Mountains—not unlike Char's Mont Ventoux, the dominant figure in a setting clearly as moral as it is physical. Thus the water springing from its source, seen upland, is its chosen image, combining both the lofty and the eternally nourishing aspects. Elsewhere, Char refers to the *oeil* of that mountain spring: because, as he explains, the eye awakens first. Then the source and the mountain merge; the mountain lake partakes of the height and distance and nobility of snow, and also of the human warmth of the hamlet, neither a city nor a town, but a small and chosen place, for a few beings ("quelques-uns"), like a double setting in the mind. The convergence of lofty situation and chosen companionship may remind the reader, even here, of that topman's perch, above the ordinary landscape and yet not quite apart. "Être parmi" ["To be among,"] reads Char's commentary on the painter Sima, as in the French translation of Heidegger: the expression should not be overlooked.

This poem, intense with meditation past and future, holds in itself the profile of a mountain and of a life, the depth of a spring and the clarity of a moral water: all are marked by suffering. But the poet no longer presents himself obliquely, as in his earlier poems, but full face, for a re-examination that is his and also ours, in the reading.

L'ETOILE DE MER

Dans le foyer de ma nuit noire
Une étincelle provocante
Heurta le tablier de cuir
Que je gardais par habitude
Autour de mes reins désoeuvrés.

Sans doute un mot bas de Cassandre,
Utile à quel avenir?
Fallait-il qu'il se révélât
Entre cinq de mes différences,
Au terme d'une parabole

De mensonge et de vérité?
Se protéger est acte vil.

Lève la tête, artisan moite
A qui toute clarté fut brève!
Cette source dans le ciel,

Au poison mille fois sucé,
N'était pas lune tarie

Mais l'étoile frottée de sel,
Cadeau d'un passant de fortune.

THE SEA STAR

In the hearth of my dark night
A provocative spark
Struck the leather apron
I used from habit to keep
About my idled loins.

Doubtless Cassandra's murmur,
Useful for what future?
Had it to be revealed
Between five of my differences,
At the outcome of a parable

Of falsehood and truth?
To protect oneself is lowly.

Lift your head, damp craftsman,
For whom all clarity was brief!
This spring in the sky,

Its poison a thousand times savored,
Was not a moon exhausted,

But the salt-touched star,
Gift of one chancing by.[7]

Dated February 1977, the second poem is constructed about the forge. The tempering of metal and the melting of iron are frequent motifs throughout Char's entire work, from the forge of the heart in "Le Devoir" ["Duty"], which leads to the firing of a young boy's temper and to the fury of the resistance, to the planet in *La Nuit talismanique*, tempered at the edge of a constellation "shivering in space." Not only the forge, but the oven too. The poet, says Char, cuts short his civilities to be there when the bread is ready to be removed, for creation takes precedence over all that is less essential. Even though the limbs are idled from those duties, the striking force, as at a poetic anvil is never-ending: "Frapper le silex à l'aube" ["To strike the flint at dawn"], we read in *Aromates chasseurs*, "s'opposer au flot des mots" ["to oppose ourselves to the flow of words," AC, 22]. Only the essential is ever worth preserving. In "L'Absent," the image is alchemical and transcends forge and oven. The presence felt here is again that of the absent brother:

> *Ce frère brutal mais dont la parole était sûre, patient au sacrifice, diamant et sanglier, ingénieux et secourable, se tenait au centre de tous les malentendus tel un arbre de résine dans le froid inalliable . . . Nous dormirons dans l'espérance, nous dormirons en son absence, puisque la raison ne soupçonne pas que ce qu'elle nomme, à la légère, absence, occupe le fourneau dans l'unité.*

> This brutal brother but whose word was true, steadfast in the face of sacrifice, diamond and wild boar, ingenious and helpful, held himself in the center of all misunderstandings like a resinous tree in the cold permitting no alloy . . . . We shall sleep in hope, we shall sleep in his absence, reason not suspecting that what it names, thoughtlessly, absence, dwells within the crucible of unity. (RC, 52–53)

The uncompromising figure of the examiner is also superimposed upon this poem, as the absent brother sets his back, "lost in time," against the lies and pettiness of a present age. The figure remains, as unmistakable witness to an indelible companionship between poet and reader.

Like the figure of the absent one, the narrator in the present poem has none of the traits of a hostage, cannot be compromised or bargained with, "admits of no alloy." The immediate future of the poet's work itself remains open to question in the poem, for if the limbs are idled here, and the night is somber, still the single spark links this text to the fire and lightning of *L'Effroi la joie*, to the "explosion in us" of "Victoire éclair" ["Lightning Victory"], and beyond it, to Orion's constellation; at this point, the passages in Char's work are strikingly vertical. The pattern of figure and ground is reversed from that of the early poems, as the forge is now of space itself. Already in *Aromates chasseurs* of 1975, the context is a meteoric one: Orion's countenance is blackened by the calcinated iron ("Evadé d'archipel" ["Escaped from the Archipelago"], RC, 284–85) and he plunges downward. The upward passage is already predicted within the same text, in Cassandra's whisper. That Orion will be received above after his time below, we know from "Orion's Reception" (RC, 284–85). His eloquence ("Eloquence d'Orion," AC, 43) is that of a "monde profond" in which the chosen figure is at once a starfish and an ocean star. The human hand appearing here, its five fingers displaying their difference—the form seeming to arise through correspondence with the starfish—is the agent of transformation and of passage, from hearth, forger's apron, and human work, eventually to the sky. This hand is never raised to protect, but only to strike the silex at dawn; a creative force and an agent of selection as well as transformation, it guides us in the text.

Nothing in the poem speaks of exhaustion: the light appears inexhaustible, although there is a trace of tears. The salt has touched the star—as the sea touches the starfish—and even the source, but only serves to deepen and, as it were, to humanize them. If we follow the track of the stars and of light itself in Char's work, from the fire of Artine, interwoven there with the image of water in the dream atmosphere, to the hostilities waged by the stars in the forest of "Pénombre" ["Penumbra"], RC, 78–79, to the single and simple candle of Madeleine before her vigil lamp, in de La Tour's plan of light and dark,[8] to the radiant universal night of "Possessions extérieures" ["Exterior Possessions"], RC, 212–13, we will find them leading back and upward to that constellation, as in a triumphal return voyage, toward the salt-touched star of this luminous poem, where the passage from human to celestial imagery is both coherent and moving.

But such a passage of vertical imagery deserves at least one more backward glance, one more reflection toward the breadth of another epoch and another art, the kind of correspondence one might call horizontal. Char's poem on "Courbet: les casseurs de cailloux" ["Courbet: The Stonebreakers"][9] from *Dehors la Nuit est gouvernée*, relates an older to a younger man as they work on a road in ruins; that picture sheds on other poems a different clarity, as "L'Etoile de mer" in its turn confers retrospectively on the Courbet canvas, even as on the corresponding text, a more visible depth. For the passerby in the poetry of Char, the brightness of the flashes in correspondence is lasting, in the net of their own self-examining.

The Courbet poem also has its most basic preoccupation in work, its accessories and accidental scenes. The wine bottle for lunchtime resting has been put to the side in the straw, where a few feathers are mixed in: "Sable paille ont la vie douce le vin ne s'y brise pas" ["Sand, straw, have a gentle life, wine doesn't shatter in them," RC, 38–39]. The young girls passing by barefooted at lunchtime are just at the age of maturity: but their chatter undermines the potential dignity of their situation: "Le sang bien souffert tombe dans l'anecdote de leur légèreté" ["Blood fitly suffered falls in talkative lightness"]; the contrast is made with the petty nastiness of the community at large. Just so, in "Le Réviseur," the pettiness of the daily world renders the lofty perch and the separate vision necessary. The habit of the leather apron is just such a detail in "L'Etoile de mer," which, like the Courbet poem, moves on in the second stanza to the essential of the work, the action of the laboring and creative hand. Distant from the small talk and gossip of the commune, the road workers, pictured by Courbet and then by Char, are better off and at ease, paradoxically, on the devastated path as they become the agents of metamorphosis: "Nous dévorons la peste du feu gris dans la rocaille" ["In the rock we devour the grey fire's plague," RC, 38–39]. Thus the heart of the dark night glimpsed in *La Nuit talismanique* seems the essential setting even now, when the landscape might seem most ruined, and the hand most idle. The thirst felt in the Courbet poem—real as it works against prettiness and artifice and implicit in the corresponding recent text—is a good one, as it corresponds to the spiritual side of the labor, calling for the deepest sources to nourish not only the outer work but the inner life.

As in "L'Etoile de mer," the final stanza of the Courbet poem makes visible the metamorphosis. After the human toil and human thirst ("Et l'aigreur de la soif tassée aux genoux" ["And thirst's sharp taste amassed in our knees"], the stones are split apart and the work heretofore of dust leads directly to the celestial "source." The spark is struck, and after the dryness of labor, a liquid image of renascence—in one case, the oil, and in the other, the spring—will be visible in the heavens:

Fils cette nuit nos travaux de poussière
Seront visibles dans le ciel
Deja l'huile du plomb ressuscite.

Son, tonight, our works of dust
Will be visible in the sky
Already oil returns to life from lead.
(RC, 38–39)

The strength of the human hand when it is devoted to whatever work it undertakes, and at whatever spiritual or physical cost—tears or sweat—as we have already learned in Char's poetry and learn again in "L'Etoile de mer," is that it forms a bridge between earth and sky, between works of dust and the resurrection on which the poem of the stonebreakers ends. The hand gathers, mediates, and bestows life, as in the poem "Lutteurs" ["Wrestlers"]: "Dans le ciel des hommes, le pain des étoiles me sembla ténébreux et durci, mais dans leurs mains étroites je lus la joute de ces étoiles en invitant d'autres: émigrantes du pont encore rêveuses; j'en recueillis la sueur dorée, et par moi la terre cessa de mourir" ["In the sky of men, the star's bread seemed to me shadowy and hardened, but in their narrow hands I read the joust of these stars calling others, emigrants from the deck, still dreamy; I gathered their golden sweat, and through me the earth ceased to die," RC, 226–27].[10]

Unobtrusively, the correspondence between age and youth, here between father and son, or between older brother and younger as in

"L'Absent," or between the poet who remains and his reader, passing by, permits the teaching of a lesson, precisely, in the passage:

> *"Fils, cette nuit nos travaux . . ." ("Les Casseurs . . .")*
> *"Lève la tête, passant pauvre . . ." ("L'Etoile de mer")*

The spark might have seemed to offer only the briefest of clarities, and the poet might have seemed only mortal, his illumination only partial: but both poems transcend earth for sky, in its most human sense. Age teaches what it has learned at great cost and is learning still, as the poorest of passersby learns the value of a spark and, perhaps, of a meteor ("This considerable passerby," said Mallarmé of Rimbaud),[11] and as the son, his knee bent to the ground in the painting, learns the final destiny of his toil. That the figure of the father does not face us is appropriate to the sense of mystery kept even in the plainest affairs. ("The heart of night should not be set afire . . .")[12] That the poet should pass on to us his lesson of an inexhaustible light, even in the midst of nocturnal dread and secrecy retained, and that the stone split apart should yield the secret of rebirth—for who has taught the father?—are matters for gratitude.

Orion, Char's chosen self-figuration, speaks eloquently indeed; yet, unlike what we might first have supposed, he does not speak only for himself. To be sure, the people among whom he has been sent have an "esprit et estomac mitoyens," a middling mind and mediocre courage; to be sure, they lose the essential of events. But the poet has forged and tried out those songs of rebellion that now return. Their fiery metal takes its ardor from his grief, tempers its roughness in tears: "Métal rallumé sans cesse de ton chagrin, ils me parvenaient humides d'inclémence et d'amour" ["Metal relit ceaselessly from your grief, they reached me damp with inclemency and with love," AC, 43]. The forge is not, will not be, idle, even if it seems so. The poet will keep his leather apron about him and pass on his lesson.

The page in which Orion dwells finally among men is situated, as in *Aromates chasseurs*, on the edge of a stream, which is now seen to converge with a mountain lake. As the Courbet vision informs the passage ending on a word of renewed hope, "ressuscite," just so, the poem of a star and of a water ends with salt, an image of resurrection after the passage made by suffering, related both to sweat and tears. "J'avais vécu": the poem narrates itself as a lived past, now repassing.

SONGS OF A PASSERBY

En dépit du froid glacial qui, à tes débuts, t'a traversé, et bien avant ce qui survint, tu n'étais qu'un feu inventé par le feu, détroussé par le temps, et qui, au mieux, périrait faute de feu renouvelé, sinon de la fièvre des cendres inhalées.

In spite of the glacial cold, which, in your beginnings, crossed through you, and well before what was to come, you were only a fire invented by fire, robbed by time, and which would at best perish for lack of renewed fire, if not from the fever of ashes inhaled. (CB, 35)

In 1976 Char brought out a small pamphlet whose title the critic or reader might well adopt, *Faire du chemin avec . . .* [*To walk along with*, . . . or then, *To make headway with . . .*] followed by three dots to indicate continuation. The epigraph of the volume, taken from "The Return of the Sire de Nesle" by Melville (who has much in common with Char) reads certainly like a return: "My tower at last! These rovings end, / Their thirst is slaked in larger dearth: / The yearning infinite recoils, / For terrible is earth."[13] And yet the text begins with a celebration of motion itself, and above all of openness: "Nous faisons nos chemins comme le feu ses étincelles. Sans plan cadastral" ["We make our paths like the fire its sparks. With no surveyor's map," FC, 1]. These lines, although their context is gravely altered, are found again in *Chants de la Balandrane* (1977). As the odd title has many meanings, each called forth, says Char, as from the well of our hearts, so, in the reader's mind, the passage and its fiery metaphor may seem to be lit by an earlier fire, and the open path, to be nourished by a preceding question in *Aromates chasseurs* of 1975: ". . . nous sommes une étincelle à l'origine inconnue qui incendions toujours plus avant. Ce feu, nous l'entendons râler et crier, à l'instant d'être consumés? Rien, sinon que nous étions souffrants, au point que le vaste silence, en son centre, se brisait." ". . . we are a spark, of origin unknown, burning always forward. Do we hear this fire in its death rattle and its cry, at the moment when we are consumed? Nothing, except that we were suffering, so much that the vast silence was breaking at its center," (AC, 34).[14]

Now the path the reader takes, or then makes here, is quite clear in its contour, and intends to remain close, in its spirit, to the *éclair nourri* or the full flash of Char's preceding work. The *éclat* and the *éclair*, like a double flash of lightning coursing through the great body of the earlier texts, are completed by the *étincelle*, the spark of this fire now always balanced by the frost or the snow in increasing accumulation upon the Mediterranean poet's oddly "Nordic" visage, as in the "Siberian Note" whose forward-burning spark was just quoted. The fire is built precisely in the face of that increasing exterior chill, and must itself then include an exterior as well as an interior way: "In spite of the glacial cold," says the poet, "you were only a fire invented by fire." The path is passionate with difficulty and moral ardor. From the beginning, each of the poems—and all are poems of passage—is both ardent and frozen. All include at their moments of greatest intensity the paradoxical convergence the surrealists taught us to stress, and yet take us beyond that point, on another sort of journey entirely. I have chosen to indicate here a few steps along one way of that journey, seen by one reader admittedly partial.[15]

Landmarks of fire might be taken as the frame in which these few comments are to be inscribed—a fireside path, then, because the hearth leads as if naturally to the stars but also to the snow, and the outer road leads just as naturally back again to the hearth or then the forge, where the poetic craft is worked in a central *locus*. Less by system than by intuition, but that at least ideally, trained as the eye is trained, on one image, as Bachelard would have it, on this most provocative of images, or on the convergence of fire and water, the latter in the form of snow or ice. Yet in a text that once concluded the path opened by the fire's spark, everything is at last acknowledged to end in ashes, to be, in fact, *sung*—as these are songs of the Balandrane—sung in ashes, both of the stars and of ourselves. We cannot fail then to remember this early scene, whose warmth endures even as the songs will.

Now from the outset of the volume, the setting is seen to take on a reddish tinge even in the boxwood, preparing an ardent path visually and imaginatively, a sort of protection or talisman against the banal, against that conversation of the multitude with anyone, "de tous avec chacun," which may at times seem to have no resonance. Fire is thus suggested in vivid hue, and the question it raises is implicitly posed to each of us—what kind of conversation can we carry on in this context, before and with these poems whose unique ardor could be betrayed by a discourse misshapenly set, badly phrased, wrongly seen? A possible answer is provided within the text of Char's own upbringing:

> *J'ai été élevé parmi les feux de bois, au bord de braises qui ne finissaient pas cendres. . . . L'hiver favorisait mon sort. Les bûches tombaient sur cet ordre fragile maintenu en suspens par l'alliance de l'absurde et de l'amour. Tantôt m'était soufflé au visage l'embrasement, tantôt une âcre fumée. Le héros malade me souriait de son lit lorsqu'il ne tenait pas clos ses yeux pour souffrir. Auprès de lui, ai-je appris à rester silencieux? A ne pas barrer la route à la chaleur grise? A confier le bois de mon coeur à la flamme qui le conduirait à des étincelles ignorées des enclaves de l'avenir? Les dates sont effacées et je ne connais pas les convulsions du compromis.*

> I was raised among wood fires, at the edge of embers which never ended as ashes. . . . Winter was favorable to my fate. The logs were falling on that fragile order held in suspense by the alliance of the absurd and of affection. Now a flame was breathed into my face, and then a bitter smoke. The sick hero smiled at me from his bed when his eyes were not closed in suffering. Near him, did I learn to remain silent? Not to close off the road to the grey heat? To confide the wood of my heart to the flame which would lead it on to the sparks still unknown by the future's enclaves? The dates have been wiped out and I do not know the convulsions of compromise. (CB, 23)

The order was always fragile, always temporary as the logs shifted about under a human hand and by their own weight—this arrangement like that of the poem itself, that other "alliance de l'absurde et de l'amour." To preserve the fragility, another question often suffices, and thus the opening text of the two-page poem "Sound of a Match" in the new volume is presented as questioning and even self-questioning in that scene, from so long ago and now so present. What did the poet learn then about confidence and openness: not to mistrust the flame as guide to the future, even though as yet only in its first spark? This dying father we saw once in the opening passage of Char's talismanic night, that he passed as through an insomnia, through which his reader is made to pass, in the fullest working out of those rites of passage of the poem we have at last learned in this poetry. There too this tireless refusal of compromise and the perils such refusal entails had to be learned by reader or by poet, each passing again over the threshold implicit once more in these pages—the "seuil" best seen in the poem of that name, where the voyager-become-host welcomes his friends from across the horizon. But here Char passes first, from the fire of the heart and the scene of his youth, with the sick and heroic father, to the moral flame and a future trial. On the verso of this page, in italics, stands the response to the poet's own question:

N'ayant que le souffle, je me dis qu'il sera aussi malaisé et incertain de se retrouver plus tard au coin d'un feu de bois parmi les étincelles, qu'en cette nuit de gelée blanche, sur un sentier ossu d'étoiles infortunées.

Having only breath, I tell myself it will be as uncomfortable and as uncertain to find myself later at the side of a wood fire among the sparks as in this night of white frost, on a bony path of unfortunate stars. (CB, 24)

Since Char's earliest poems, we have understood that breath is the sole and prized possession of the poet—"Respiration," an early poem, in which the mountain climber acknowledges his breathing as his only riches. Breath forces the passage, from in to out, from comfort to adventure, from the interior fire to the frozen night path, strewn with what might be the cooled remains of fallen meteorites—those "étoiles infortunées." Orion, fallen as a meteor in Char's poetic mythology, returns ceaselessly to our minds with his face blackened by his fall, his choice that of remaining here among the human while the stars whisper above him and above us all:

Orion,
Pigmenté d'infini et de soif terrestre,

. . .

Les traits noircis par le fer calciné

Orion,
Colored by the infinite and by earthly thirst,

. . .

His features blackened by calcinated iron

(AC, 9)

We remember how in "L'Etoile de mer," a poem facing the passage of sparks with which this brief commentary begins, one "provoking" spark falls from the heavens into the forge worked, like a poetic gift, during the black night to illuminate the rest of the way. Orion fallen and choosing to remain or the poet at his work signaled by the sky—both are in the same vertical line of exchange, up and down, and that line is included again within the line of these poems, where the inner fire of the hearth is to the human and earthly what the outer path of the frozen night is to the heavens. All the directions converge here, as the red of the flame calls forth, onto the path of our visual imagination, the white of the frost. The confusing flame and the ardent heart of the child are transposed to the realm beyond and outside, but the inner determination remains the guide to the outer path, marked by a strong sense of the moral venture, of the trial and the discovery of the self, in a fiery crossing, as the poet speaks of the path.

But in the long run, and in face of the devouring flames, despite the most courageous venture of the most uncompromising poet, only the book will survive, and by a passage through another hand. A page is awakened, read by an eye ablaze, and held in passion: "Vivant là où son livre raidi se trouve. Et doublement vivant si une main ardente ouvre le livre à une page qui someillait" ["Living where his hardened book is found. And doubly living if an ardent hand should open the book to a page which was dozing," CB, 22–28]. In *La Nuit talismanique* another hand held the candle, as by a spontaneous gesture; here the hand has absorbed the illumination and taken on its own heat. But before the book is established in its rigidity, a simple slate must be inscribed in all its accidental thereness. It has the fragility of that initial order of logs in the fireplace, a temporary arrangement, an inner correspondence with human contingency: "La parole écrite s'installe dans l'avènement des jours comptés, sur une ardoise de hasard" ["The written word takes up its dwelling in the coming of days, as they are counted, on a slate of chance," CB, 30]. Suffered, this word leaves a trace of red, is in fact "the bindweed of blood drawn from the rock itself"—the slate is held out for fate to mark, so that between the inner flame and the external path there may stretch sufficient space for ardor and for moral transit. As the cycle is completed, from domestic hearthside to the outer stars, and now at last from the outer frozen path to the interior experience, the discourse finds its frame: "Toi, une façon de neige intérieure révèle à tes suivants la fin de tes attachements en même temps que la conversion de ton exil" ["An interior snow reveals you to those who follow, the end of your attachments and the simultaneous conversion of your exile," CB, 63]. The ardent hand about to wake the slumbering pages will discover one day the entirety of the path.

Exile itself—which has included the descent of Orion from the heavens and has worn down the trail strewn with remains of meteors—exile itself is converted in its sense, and reintegration is assured after the rites of passage and of liminarity. The threshold crossed for the outer journey is crossed once more: "Yes, we make our paths as the fire its sparks," and with as little stringency in our system, for the path that was to be completed for poet and reader was plainly the path of the self. "Devoir se traverser pour arriver au port!" ["Having to traverse oneself in order to arrive in port!" CB, 67]. And, according to the title following, the talisman is saved even from the flame: "The Scarab Is Saved in Extremis." "L'étoile retardataire vient à son tour d'éclater" ["The refractory star just exploded in its turn," CB, 68], the text begins. Stars burst apart then, and the fire is renewed, embers as well as ashes. On the brazier, it continues to hail, and the interior snow falls in this ardent, private adventure, in this inner landscape. Thus we, as well as the poet, are returned after our own passage through the text to the hearth, the profound source of the imagery and the guide to the future paths held within the self, outer and inner, like Orion descended and still apparent in the sky. Like a fire died down but still aflame, or a star exploded, like a pulverized poem. Throughout the talismanic night of the self or of the text, as through the most matinal of clarities, the reader may be guided by some ardent gaze, felt or imagined, or some hand not his own, may in fact, be "walking along with" whatever referent he might most wish to place at the end of that expression, open as it is meant to be, and must, in all discretion, remain. But Char's final admonition is always toward freedom: once, not so long ago, we may have read his concluding words as if they had been addressed to himself only, but they reveal themselves, upon re-reading, to concern themselves also with our present and future choosing, of a word and of a way: "Tu tiens de toi tes chemins, / Aussi leur personne pensive" ["From yourself you take your paths / And their thoughtful being," CB, 78].

These poems then make their way, as the others before them, upward and down, outward and in, and—as a fire makes its sparks—forward. In Char's texts, voice and essential echo meet along the way, "la voix" and "la voie," vibrant in their convergence, in these songs for a thoughtful path.

JACQUES GARELLI
Opening and Breach

THE HOLE IN THE CLOTH

. . . sur cette oeuvre repliée, face
à vous, je romps . . .

. . . bent over this work, facing you,
I break off . . .

JACQUES GARELLI, *Brèche*[1]

For the poet or critic who believes that the poem has its source in initial nothingness, in the gaping hole of Non-Sense between future and past, empty sign and useless signified, what can be its nature and status? How is it to be related to or inserted in the moment, which already carries a grave fault, a divergence in itself? In what light can it and its metacommentary be seen, if not as a language inappropriate, incorrect, and worse still, inanimate?

. . . ce corps
devenu par long balbutiement erreur
de soi-même texte jeté à vif poème ce
mort à soi de cendres . . .

. . . this body
become by a lengthy stammering an error
of itself text thrown living poem
this death to itself of ashes . . .

(LP and LPB, 20)

It is one thing to assume, as I did in my comments on "The Breach of the Poem," that the right to knowledge, whether for the poet or for the critic or philosopher, has been abandoned, together with the faith in the concept or even the desirability of the complete, and even instant, entry by the poetic word to a privileged place and a language set apart. It is far worse to see that language, poetic or not, deprived of a precise or satisfying parallel to the real, to see it, uncoincident and unable even to evaluate: to experience a slippage, between it and what it would touch, grasp, or measure: "Savoir que nos tables ne sont pas exactes" ["To know that our tables are not exact," LP, 16]. Language may be parallel to our mental model, as it is not fit for the most minimal demands of accuracy, significance, or direction.

So the poem must become equivalent to that readjusted state of things. The poem, says Garelli, offers us a universe never whole but rent asunder, never standing level, but always slightly askew. When its weave of sounds is torn, the exposure reveals only slightly the object or idea beyond, each word crooked, half-ajar, on a meaning often confused, or then irrelevant to the concern of the poem. He gives a specific orientation to the discussion of the hole as it is recognized and signaled, as it is made or opens spontaneously in the *stuff* of poetry, corresponding to the principle of negation gaping open in the heart of being. For if "the poetic work renders present that which opens a presence," it is not by means of any magic or even lyric incantation to completion or wholeness—no hymns to the absolute—but rather by the initial phonetic explosion of the word as well as by its semantic plurality; neither betrays by a fatal overoptimism the fault so clearly seen. Explosion and plurality are noncommittal as far as value is concerned: "Éclatez, les mots!" ["Words, burst apart!" B, 16].

EXPLOSION AS PROJECT

The fissure detected in being (without the dramatic glory of existential division, being a simple phenomenological perception of slippage), the inappropriateness felt, in the word, the faults and lacks of the mind and its surroundings, and in their correspondence, all are inserted in a temporal topos clearly marked out on the scanned surface of the poem. Time—even in the time of the poem—tears asunder, savaged like the eye sacrificed or bleeding, which haunts

Garelli's *Lieux précaires* [*Precarious Places*], yet is redeemed still by a sight to come (the "oeil futur" or the "oeil . . . du voyant," [the "future eye" and the eye of the "seer"]), or by a unique eye of the Cyclops, powerful and singular. A belief in the unique value of each moment depending on its own profound separation as it is pulled toward past and future underlies Garelli's conception of the poem as a distinct and irreplaceable point in space, becoming, in the time of reading, also our moment and our place, then by implication, our passage. Of the poem as our single temporal-spatial obsession and the inevitable landscape for our self-knowledge, Garelli says simply: "Il hante notre espace car il est notre temps" ["It haunts our space for it is our time," PA, 54]. Yet the poetic word, like the transitional moment rent apart in its fore-word and after-word, is prey to a desperate dispersion even more extreme than the temporal rending, an "explosion diasporique de ses extases présentes" ["explosion in diaspora of its present ecstasies," GP, 164]. Furthermore, lest it be thought that an explosive force is only the inevitable prelude to the text, a setting-in-action merely benign in its intensification of the poetic project, we should consider this quotation from Jacques Lacan placed at the threshold of *Les Dépossessions* as a sign of its extreme seriousness and excess, like a passage by blood and fire:

> *Ce qui se démontre dans l'espace imaginaire du poète, vaut métaphysiquement ce qui se passe de plus sanglant dans le Monde, car c'est cela qui dans le Monde fait couler le sang.*
>
> What is shown in the imaginary space of the poet is the metaphysical equivalent of bloodiest happenings in the World, for it is that which within the World causes the blood to flow. (LD, 9)

This act of linguistic birth is no less violent than a physical one and cannot be transcribed except in the least forgiving of terms. All the forceful gravity of *La Gravitation poétique* is summed up in the final paragraph describing the birth of the poem in the brutality of breach and the ugliness of a hideous passage, where Lacan's expression "fait couler le sang" is replaced by something still worse:

> *Mais au sein du langage, l'irruption sauvage d'une brèche d'où coule l'inépuisable hémorragie des mots truqués, tronqués . . . .*

> But at the heart of language, the savage irruption of a breach through which there floods the inexhaustible hemorrhage of deformed and mutilated words . . . . (GP, 213)

The words exploding are mutilated in a savagery often beyond any recognizable sense, offensive to a poetic sensitivity that would pride itself on subtlety, accustom itself to nuance. Exclamation points punctuate the page, ripping holes into that surface ordinarily smooth from the typographic point of view. Speech, discontinuous and harsh, tears into the tissue of former calm, gouging out its exact place, in an operation often unwelcome and always uncomfortable: words make holes in silence itself. Thus, the "exploded" being of the poet projects itself (*expresses* itself) in a ritual irremediably destructive of the tranquilly efficacious or merely functional gestures of a neutral discourse, "prenant appui sur l'explosion étoilée du langage . . ." ["relying on the stellar explosion of language," PA, 54].

Knowing that the word in poetry can never be the perfect correspondent for the external object, that the poetic image may never "serve" any sense, historical or social, the poet remains intimately and necessarily preoccupied with the mere sounds of the poem in its making, this irreducible being forcing itself into presence, a linguistic world creating itself: "es weltet," said Heidegger, and Garelli responds, "le monde se mondifie" ["the world worlds"]. Explosion first occasions the verbal landscape characterized "par ses décisions brusques . . . , par ses sauts . . . , par ses secousses, par ses insoutenables convulsions" ["by the unexpected appearance of its wild hiccoughs, by its brusque decisions . . . , by its leaps . . . by its shaking, its unbearable convulsions," PA, 86]. The idea of rupture is repeatedly reinforced within the text, from the individual word or image in its phonetic, syntactic, and semantic functions, through the tempo, the N.I.A.S.T.V. ("devoid of all ontic reality / . . . the Intentional Kernel of Variable Tensions with Sounded Articulations," GP, 198).[2] Garelli considers the poetic image neither referential nor emotional, only an audible condensation of temporality making itself ["expression sonore du temps se faisant"]. The text is simply the temporal ground of what is experienced through the material structure of the word, and this is to suffice as presence, and as poetry. For example, the word tree ["arbre"] is used not for any such connotations as the linking of earth and sky or the stability of its trunk, or the rustling of its leaves, but rather for the audible abruptness, for its sharp edge rupturing the poem's surface with its aggressive interjection: "arrr-brrr," so that in the sounded material of language the broken surface can then freshly stand apparent to the perception. Similarly, the uneven course of tempo and syntax stresses, as does the sound, the extreme irregularities of texture and the violent interruptions of thought that it encourages in the reader. Attention is directed to the push and pulsations of thought itself, with its "interventions of nothingness," as Paul Claudel says; Garelli now uses, by a reverse procedure, the lacunae in language as the foundation for mental experience, the renewal of imagination. The poetic text is meant to disturb and thereby re-create, by its phonetic sharpness, explosive precision and jagged profile, a vivid observation and presence, against the laziness of habit. As the Dadaists maintained that thought was made in the mouth or by the automatic impulse of the hand, so Garelli insists on similar birth for poetry in an "automatic and explosive release" totally devoid of mysticism: "Né de la gorge, par son rythme lacuneux, le poème fonde" ["Born in the throat, by its rhythm of gaps, the poem establishes," B, 63].

WORD IN MOTION

ouvrir un monde
to open a world

JACQUES GARELLI, *Prendre appui*

Within the punctured surface corresponding to and encouraging a discontinuous consciousness, a certain coherence is retained in the "self-moving emptiness" of the poem seen as open to the sky, its fissures taken as its meaning. In Garelli's conception, convincing in its very bareness, all things open upon themselves—words, stories, windows, and the work, which "secretes" its own history, its landscape, and its situation. This is the other side of the negative emptiness "eating away" at the words already used like a devouring void (LP, 17): Garelli's disruptive and dramatic word effects its own *auto-constitution*, its sense and situation undetermined a priori. *Prendre appui* [*To Take Support*], his most developed statement, in poetry and on presence, leaves open in its title the manner and agent of support. It ends in openness also, with a brief and powerful invocation that is at once a hope, a serious commitment, and a stubborn witness to the mobile self-determination of the word in the self-exposure of its passage: "Que la parole fasse venir à la parole, le temps, le site, le lieu. Qu'elle s'ouvre sur elle-même et établisse le dire en sa demeure." ["May speech bring to speech time, site, place. May it open upon itself and establish saying where it dwells" PA, 96].

PLACE AND TIME

> *Lieu de rencontre . . .*
> Meeting place . . .
> JACQUES GARELLI, *Brèche*

In the text, no continuity is assured. "Des fonds cloisonnés dressent les remparts d'un langage mouvant" ["Walled-up depths raise the ramparts of a moving language," LP, 31]. Although those compartments with their vertical marks, as much the indications of lines and margins as of walls, are seen in proximity to a language in motion, they appear from a distance to reject both light and space:

> *Maisons d'angle aux cloisons opaques*
> *Qui ouvrent opaques sur d'autres cloisons*
> *Jardins clos*
> *Jardins d'hiver*
>
> Houses at an angle with opaque separations
> Opening opaque on other separations
> Closed gardens
> Winter gardens (LP, 61–62)

The texts of *Lieux précaires* [*Precarious Places*], offering a risk for the mind and the body of poetry, are as a whole dedicated to the problems of enclosure, separation, memory, and time. The positive note in the title "La Pluie belliqueuse du souviendras" ["The Warlike Rain of You Will Remember"] is haunted by the negative expression of memory annulled: "nulle souvenance," echoing across the landscape to which the title refers, so that the memory of memory, accepted or negated, sets the tone for an investigation of time and temporal distance.

Initially, the references to time are as oblique as they are extensive. To perceive them clearly and in their individual setting, the attentive reader must disengage them from their accessory litanic variants, diverse phonetic vestments covering the temporal obsession: time takes on many guises. The importance of patience—signaled time and again by the poet—is made clear, for the reader is to listen, and to time itself: "Il prête l'oreille à l'écoute du temps" ["He lends an ear to the listening of time," LP, 52]. The series of phonetically associated terms: "j'attends," "tant," "l'attente," "tente," "le temple," in all of which "le temps" can be heard, begins, strikingly, with patience itself: "J'attends" ("I await," LP, 47). Then this imposed waiting stretches throughout the twelve pages of the poem "making itself" in time, only to end by destroying the instant elaborated with such patience:

> *J'at*tends *sans plaisir sans remords sans repos*
> . . .
> *J'at*tends *l'instant*
> . . .
> *J'at*tends
> . . .
> *L'att*en*te n'a-t-elle pas été att*en*te de tous* temps?
> *L'histoire pour toujours a saboté le* temps.
>
> I await without pleasure without remorse without rest
> . . .
> I await the moment
> . . .
> I await
> . . .

Has not waiting been waiting for all time?
History has forever sabotaged time. (LP, 58)

These phonetic variations on the theme of time occupying the very time of the text working itself out, form the sections between which the stuff of the poem must unroll, in the temporal *lacunae*: now "temps" as "temple" will be cracked in its monolithic structure of traditional strength before expectation yields to poetry. "Le temple lézardé avec ses vestiges de lierre" ["The cracked temple with its remains of ivy," LP, 53].

Nevertheless, the lament concerning the deformations and the irrelevance of language is grave, for the suspicion of uselessness corrodes poetic language:

L'image le jeu métaphore première
Paroles décalées imperceptibles torsions
Ces signes ne mènent à rien
Ce discours de même

The image the game first metaphor
Words out of fit imperceptible twists
These signs lead to nothing
Like this discourse (LP, 66)

Even if the temporal divisions of the text are shown to be temporary, the long trial of words ("essayer les mots") may lead nowhere, except to itself, a solution acceptable or not. The poet leaves the way open for both answers:

Encore un mot: ce poème, je l'aime. On a vécu à deux. Comme d'autres, on se perdra. Il ne conduit à rien, sauf peut-être à lui-même. Parti de moi, pour sûr, il est vide. Ne l'est pas.

One more thing: I love this poem. We have lived together. Like others, we will be lost. It leads to nothing, except perhaps to itself. Having started with me, surely, it is empty. Is not. (B, 27)

The final hesitation is grave and unresolvable, and the final promise of memory possibly implied in the title ("Souviendras") is inefficacious before the doubt assailing the foundations of speech.

A solitary gesture ends the group of poems, absorbing the enclosure by a closing-off into darkness, into the obscurity of a willingly arrested text "Phrases barrées [qui] comme les murs arrêtent les regards" ["Sentences struck out (which) like walls arrest one's gaze," PA, 74] and a half-veiled acknowledgment that the individual game has been badly played (the "jeu mal noué" yielding, by phonetic suggestion, a "je" or a "jeu mal joué"):

Et du jeu mal noué l'incidente la strophe
Que nul à ce jour vous non plus n'écrira
Je remets la clef et je clos la porte
Barricadé vivant dans le noir

And the incident the stanza from the game
badly tied
That no one as yet nor you will write
I put the key back and I close the door
Barricaded live in the darkness (LP, 120)

The poem whose title was once meant to provide the title for the volume, "Et Neige ma raison," can be taken by a phonetic re-reading as a further question about the value of this or any text, and all the statements contained therein:

Et neige ma raison [*Et n'ai-je ma raison?*]

And snow my reason (And have I not my reason?)

For the "precarious place" is not only a possible metaphoric reference to the skier's danger in the snow, but beyond that precarious situation, a warning as to the gravity of so-called poetic speech, that word "opening on to itself." For therein the commonplace or the proverbial statement, some ordinary "lieu commun," is changed to the "lieu précaire," situated in a time that risks being swept aside by the passage of history itself.

A still more recent poem, "Le Savoir" ["Knowledge"], inquires into the basis of ontological pessimism, the ground of poetry's essential gravity. Garelli's book-length essay *La Gravitation poétique* is already a commitment to seriousness—the essay is of Heideggerian weight—but the poem "Le Savoir" plays out in the space of a very few lines a temporal drama stretching again from wait and expectation to a realization of final expendability, applicable even to poetry. Instantly and insistently, the poem strikes out at a superfluous time ("temps de trop") and at the waste of words. The text, including the following lines, is the conclusion of Garelli's *Le Recel et la dispersion* (Paris: Gallimard, 1978), p. 178.

Aucun ordre n'est venu périmé ou lisse dans les déverses absolues de la lumière . . . les chemins furent parcourus les yeux jadis visionnaires clos perturbés marginaux sur des trous . . . Il parle face aux autres rejetés de côté Blancheur immotivée repliée sur des prés rhétoriques sifflantes l'usure est dans les mots dans les bleus incendiés qui déchirent les métaux pour sûr les haches éffarées du soleil la main renversée sur un temps de trop.

No order has come elapsed or smooth in the absolute outpourings of light . . . the paths were traveled the eyes once visionary closed perturbed marginal upon holes . . . He speaks facing the others rejected on one side Unmotivated whiteness folded back on rhetorical whistling meadows depreciation is in the words in the burned blues which surely rend the metals these startled axes of the sun the hand reversed upon a useless time.

These lines can be read as a poetic manifesto or "art poétique," with all its self-referential claims; the poem cannot be structured by any order exterior to its being and so all waiting for an outside force is vain. Within its own paths, even the most sunlit of passages is interrupted and perturbed, the poet prone to violence and conscious of his gesture never fitting, but "de trop" like the time in which his expectation was situated and was deceived. His hand is useless whether played directly or reversed: the stuff of poetry is badly flawed.

Despite everything, "le chemin reste à faire" ["the path must yet be made"]. The violent breach made in the edifice of the text can be used as the path toward a new place, still uncertain, filled with a legendary resonance and an understated menace: "Il est dit que la bêche ouvrira ce ton plus haut dans le jardin; que l'arbre fleurira de pierres entre tes doigts." ["It is said that the hoe will open that higher tone in the garden; that the tree will flower with stones between your fingers," B, 47]. These gardens opened by a savage gesture, this text ruptured by uneven rhythms, guard the singular perfection of the blossomed stones figuring, in the place of danger, the precarious site of poetry. As poets like du Bouchet, Deguy, and Dupin celebrate the ascent of the mountain of the text whose incline and whose crevasses challenge and promise, Garelli celebrates the precariousness of the simple word ruptured and rupturing in its supreme harshness, its steep way. "Ici une parole qui a toujours été. Ses carrefours, multiples, ses abords, sévères." ["Here a speech which has been always. Its crossroads multiple, its approaches stern," PA, 43]. In a possible divergence from its first meaning, like those other re-readings offered here, poetic speech pronounced in its ambiguity, reveals its essential quality within its concealed name: sévères = ces vers.

The text now daydreamed as entire and spotless, a smooth surface the sun reflects upon ("Je rêve d'un poème comme d'un mur blanc" ["I dream of a poem as of a white wall,"] PA, 87), still leads to an inexplicable labyrinth whose divisions are always recognized as such, as the "cloisons" separating and inseparable from those depths self-created by pulsations of thought. "Départs des départs," these stammered partings, "des parts des des parts," are perhaps after all only the fragmentary passages in a maze and design not perfectly ordered, since the order is given by the pulsations of thought. Here place and time are telescoped, "Ici et pour toujours" ["Here and for always," LD, 30].

CLOSURE ON AN INNER SPACE

The final passage is made into a *Difficile séjour*, a "Difficult Sojourn" in space and in time, as if in response to the telescoping texts written for the sculptures of Gonzalo Fonseca, whose monumental simplicity recalls at once the Egyptian tombs and the cave dwellings, figures at once life and death. Unwaveringly serious, these poems create a bareness as irrevocable and unforgiving as any law, by "l'effroi des parois" ["the fright of the walls"], a tomb with no material escape:

Il y faut un tombeau sans ors sans recours . . .

. . .

Ramener le silence à l'instance des couleurs

A tomb is needed bare of golds of hope

. . .

To bring back silence like colors

(DS, n.p.)

The passage ends here, with the mind unhindered by such captivity as the glance of others usually enforces: "l'oeil reste sans prise sur l'esprit qui chemine" ["the eye has no hold over the spirit making its way"], and the spirit is free to wander. Such light as there is has itself an Egyptian cast to it, and only the sphinx signs these walls. Suns are plural here, and yield a potent shadow: a question as to the interaction of the human and the stone is all-pervading:

Peut-on risquer la nuit taire le bruit

. . .

Peut-on percer ce bloc où rien ne murmure rien ne s'éveille rien ne pourrit rien ne s'étend

Can one risk the night make the sound silent

. . .

Can one pierce this block where nothing murmurs nothing wakes nothing rots or extends (DS, n.p.)

The echo "nuit/bruit" sounds hollow against the smoothness of these walls, and the repetition continues, resonant with nothingness: "rien ne . . . rien ne . . . rien ne . . . rien ne . . . ." For his own descent into these walls, the poet has prepared himself by a previous passage, by a long patience whose marks have been visible before, implying all the ages of human experience, in the face of mortality and of these signifying stones: "Ainsi ai-je voyagé en boule quelques décades dans les veinures à peine explorées d'une pierre" ["Thus have I traveled curled up for some decades in the veining of a stone scarcely yet explored," DS, n.p.].

The stone is on the side of the eternal, like the caves of Lascaux, and the poet's gaze is never that of a passerby; it has rather, the profundity of the stone itself:

De tout temps cette caverne pour l'oeil un repaire . . . l'immortel y sévit s'enfonce s'envoûte . . . le bison et sa proie.

From always this cavern a lair for the eye . . . the immortal rages there sinks there is enthralled there . . . the bison and his prey. (DS, n.p.)

Linked to that of the primordial beast, the primordial power of the poet penetrates these prehistoric stones and becomes himself that other matter and its phoenix: "Moi la pierre moi la cendre un peu courbé sauvage" ["I the stone I the ashes slightly bent wild," DS, n.p.]. The monumentality of this text may be likened to that of Char's Lascaux poems; in both cases, the words are given their depth by a poet's philosophic meditation, on the bison and on Lascaux man. Bonnefoy's *Pierre écrite* and Deguy's *Tombeau de Du Bellay* have also their parallel in this womb of a stone text.

Garelli finds against the stone, and within it, his own being: "Il a réglé ses comptes avec le temps investi une raison dans les grains de la lumière rompu le partage . . ." ["He has settled his accounts with time, invested reason in the seeds of the light shattered the sharing . . . ," DS, n.p.]

At the center of one concluding fragment is the place of an interior voyage, a passage made into the architecture of the dream and the tomb, situated in the "Interlieu Intermonde" ["Between place Between world"]. It is marked by a one-line statement, of a brevity noticeable among the longer paragraphs surrounding, and says simply, "C'est la chambre" ["It's the room"]. Here, says Garelli, the immemorial body pursues its destiny, beyond its individual end, for all men and for all moments. The text is inscribed, like a poem, on the inside of the stone, a fate is chosen, and a silence meditated.

A sun is present, even within this inner passage, and may be touched: "Là du soleil à portée de la main" ["There, in the hand's reach, is the sun"]. Within the world the illumination is found, on the inside and without, now and for always.

MICHEL DEGUY
Boundary Gesture

THE POEM AS BIRTH AND THEATER

Attendre un chemin des mots
Awaiting a path from words[1]
MICHEL DEGUY, *Actes.*

Among the recent attempts made at the efficacious joining of poetic theory and practice, one of the most convincing is the series of texts Michel Deguy has devoted to the oddly self-involved nature of the poetic act. Already his meditations link, by their style, poetry to prose and self-reflection to outward concern. Refusing the distinctions ordinarily seen as holding between essay and poem, Deguy describes the latter in its self-engagement as an infinitely dense utterance tightly coiled within itself, devoid of exterior concerns. Its own referent and the sole determiner of its own ramifictions, it is first of all an object awaiting its own *diction*, an empty sign that will eventually summon its own meaning (the *signifiant* summoning the *signifié* instead of the reverse). Isolated and enclosed within a self-perpetuating complexity instead of *situated* in a historical sense, the poem is said to take its departure from a *source* or a "spring," the term already indicating the liquidity of the basic matter of language. Thus the word *ressource* closing the following text is at once a deliberate intensification, a thematic resurgence, and a reawakening of the linguistic source itself:

Objet frémissant
Signe appelant le sens
Oiseaux aimantés à
Nidifier en les branches qui s'inventent
Le poème ramifie en sa propre ressource

Object quivering
sign summoning the sense
Birds magnetized
To nest in the branches inventing themselves
The poem branches out in its own resource.

(B, 117)

Coil and spring are perfect images for the "quivering" of theory within text, the self-restraint imposed in the enclosure, and the simultaneous ongoing activity, sensed in the term "frémissant" and the carry-over of magnetic charge from the third to the fourth line: not the static product but the process.

The poem *is* not, rather it quivers in the passage of its own making. Deguy insists at once on the serious nature of the poetic act at its origin always renascent, and on its temporal status, converging in the title "Actes de naissance" ["Birth Acts"], wherein the proof given by the birth certificate passes into the birth-giving *action*.

Notwithstanding, the process is neither foolproof nor continually convincing. The spiraling linguistic act thus leads into a rapid decrescendo, the fall of lines downward upon the page corresponding in mood to a desperate inner exploration, doomed to end. The poetic act is not always a bringing forth, but may rather represent a further miring down of language in its own peculiar limits, in the search for its own depth:

Et le poème cherche un plus profond poème
Un autre sous celui-ci
Il tourne dans la place sous ce parcours
Un plus profond poème sous le poème
Qui commence mal
cet escalier fragile et défoncé sur la page

And the poem seeks a poem more profound
Another under this one
It spins in the square beneath this passage
A poem more profound under the poem

Which starts badly
this fragile staircase collapsed on the page
(B, 132)

We are, according to Deguy, in an epoch of contraction. A poem is not just its own reason, but also its own grammar, a poetry about poetry; "this *language of language* which is poetic language" (G, 112) forms a continuous syntagmatic chain by the comparison and the coappearing of what were discontinuous elements. Deguy has always been a poet of appositional consciousness, as an early, untitled text in *Poèmes de la presqu'île* testifies:

O la grande apposition du monde
un champ
de roses près d'un champ de blé et deux enfants
rouges dans le champ voisin du champ de roses
et un champ de maïs près du champ de blé et deux
saules vieux à la jointure; le chant de deux enfants
roses dans le champ de blé près du champ de roses
et deux vieux saules qui veillent les roses les blés les
enfants rouges et le maïs

Le bleu boit comme tache
L'encre blanc des nuages
Les enfants sont aussi mon
Chemin de campagne

Oh the great apposition of the world
a bed
of roses near a field of wheat and two red children
in the field next to the bed of roses
and a field of corn near the field of wheat and two
willows old at the joining; the song of two children
red in the field of wheat near the bed of roses
and two old willows which watch over the roses the
wheat the
red children and the corn

The blue drinks like a spot
The white ink of clouds
The children are also my
Country path (DEP, 17–18)

Given the will to link what might have been dispersed,[2] the evident sensitivity to sight visible in this passage, and the connected feeling explicit or implicit, which will never disappear entirely from Deguy's work, his insistence on metalanguage and on the poem as its own metaphor and theory does not imply that the poetic act is an incorporeal exercise, desiccated in a purely mental state, a sterile noncommitment to any but linguistic life. For at the very juncture of words and things, in the privileged place of metaphoric transformation, which is to say of passage, Deguy *reincorporates*, makes bodily once more, the metaphor as gesture: "The body at the center. . . . The body is first at the festival: a token of all figures, at the encounter of space and of the word, of the metaphoric parabola and the metonymic system; it is the gesture . . . to which the word is joined . . . the joining of word and gesture in their simultaneous whole. To this primary festival of gesture, to this inaugural recognition of what is required of us as ceremony, permitting our figurative speech, the poem as birth certificate bears witness" (A, 272–80). If the stress on collectivity and the stylistic solemnity remind us of Breton, the particular pointing at gesture may remind us of Artaud, freed of the tragic obsession of his own incompetence, endowed with resonance and assurance. From Deguy's double point of view as spectator or critic and poet, the poem is its own theater, where a vivid consciousness of verbal costume and linguistic role dominates both the spontaneous and the habitual. Thus the theatrical vocabulary: *Actes*, he calls one essay on the poetic, and another, *Figurations*. A recasting of tropes is among the first principles of the primary grammar contained in the poem; not only does the term "trope" refer to the systematic metamorphosis of language, but it is also reminiscent of the "tropes" of medieval theater. "Recasting" is no less theatrical. When the poem is seen to begin as a festival, pulling the words into its ritual dance, it celebrates a collective rhythm and its own individual self-discovery, through the collective experience.

Continuing the images and the suppositions of theater, Deguy recommends for the dramatic architectural structure of poetry the comparative genitive (where comparison is deliberately linked to coappearance: not only the coincidence, already mentioned, but also "coappearance" in its stagy implications. Still in a theatrical sense, he takes the words "the" and "of" as the two pillars of an expository arcade, for instance, where two nominal elements subsequently appear and are exhibited, posed, and exposed in the linguistic theater. The metaphor of spectacle, occuring always at a particular location and in a particular moment, permits the encounter of the specific and the general, of display and reflection. Set apart from the space of the prosaic, where presumably one thing goes on at once, the place of the poem is at once ambiguous and ambivalent, like some neutral ground of mediation, enabling the passage into duplicity and metamorphosis. On this stage his twin perceptions, *Jumelages*, or doublings, can be set; one action or one place is "jumelé" with another, for a dynamic play. Now the play of ambiguities, opposing poetic to prosaic passage, has a parallel in the nonprosaic play of reversed motion and reversed perception. The following examples come from a passage in the early work, *Biefs*, where the attachment of language to the exterior world is far more marked than in later works: "chutes inverses du jour, / Cygnes renversés, / nuages inversés / course inversée." [". . . Swans turned around," / "clouds inverted," / "backwards race," / and the double reversal of "inverted day fall."] Such reversed spectacles absorb and exalt: "cet envers qui nous happe et nous édifie" ["this other side which snaps us up and edifies us," B, 65], in a universe prey to sudden arrest, of light ["la lumière arrêtée"], of body, ["le corps arrêté"] and of perception itself. As with the breaking of univalent codes by duplicity or multiplicity, the reversal of vision is both breach in the code and breakthrough, and runs the risk of finding only emptiness at the center.

But the poem of the absent center, language spiraling about itself, alternates with exterior perception throughout Deguy's writing in its own self-spectacle. The "passage of emptiness here" ["le vide passant ici"] transforms all things and their perceptions into moments of absence, so many spaces of empty space ["autant d'espaces que les choses," F, 16]. The most absorbing vision is scattered, as in "la conscience éparse," consciousness loses coherence and is diffused; finally, the "I" is dissolved and watches its dissolution, as even the "je" is annulled in the sentence. Narrator, poet, observer are exiled from the spectacle, the drama, and the space of the poem.

SELF-PORTRAIT IN A PASSAGE

Le poète de profil
The poet in profile
MICHEL DEGUY, *Oui dire*

As for self-definition, the poet is given being mainly by his wandering, from his early walks in the "presqu'île" (*Poèmes de la presqu'île*) of a real landscape to the recent "Made in USA" (*Jumelage*), where the feverish pace betrays the poet more at ease with motion than emotion. The following early "self-portrait" was later chosen by Deguy as the liminary text for an anthology of his work (*Poèmes*). The poem makes a clear description of a poet of perpetual movements spared superficiality by his acknowledgment and its light irony:

Nul ne fut hanteur plus obstiné; qui mit plus de ruse, plus de résolution au service d'une hantise vaine; nul plus insistant à imiter le flux et le reflux, à devenir élément-homme, d'universelle hantise; à revenir buter, blesser obstinément contre les arbres, contre le ciel, contre la mer

None was a haunting more determined; none placed more ruse or resolution at the service of a useless obsession; none more insistent at imitating the ebb and the flow, to become an element-man, of a universal haunting; to come back to strike against, to wound the trees, the sky, the sea

(DEP, 9)

The insistent "nul" haunts the text in its own comings and goings, its vowel sound "u" repeated in the "fut," "plus," "ruse," –"ution," "une," and above all in the self-fulfilling "flux" and "reflux," followed by the generalization ["universelle"] and the stress on stubbornness ["buter"]. These stubborn repetitions are like so many blows against the obstacle sensed, where an untiring preposition itself resounds, "contre," "contre," "contre." Stubborn also, the natural elements against which the speaker pits himself in his own obstinacy, as he takes the measure of his haunts: "L'inlassable vague et l'inlassable oiseau et l'inlassable vent" ["the untiring wave and the untiring bird and the untiring wind"]. The triplet form echos the previous "contre . . . contre . . . contre" until the long sentence gradually subsides, like a wave—or in the correspondence of the natural and the human—like the exhaling of a long uninterrupted breath. The tireless sentence flows not toward some infinite but toward that which is interposed, toward that which will be stated as a boundary between sand and foam, cliff and storm: the passage is never seen as limitless.

The haunter who returns everywhere ("le revenant, partout"), the poet obsessed and obstinate, will forever be posed only at the edge of things, like a traveler, will haunt the dividing line where a "being of boundaries" ("être de lisières") overlooks the convergence of valley and plain, or, when the line is seen negatively, will find himself "stuck at the crossroads." On the formal level, in the "poem of the poem," which is also its own theory, the crossroads is also the linguistic juncture, a "charnière (pli, jointure, feuillure, brisure)" ["a hinge, pleat, joining, groove, articulation"],[3] a juncture, which is also a separation. This obsessive articulation, in its rupture and continuation, gives the poem its problematic and complicated nature. The act of the poem is a crossroads act, a drama of juncture and disjuncture.

In this passage *between*, a sort of neutral space or threshold, Deguy situates himself, between reading and writing, between lands ["jumelages"] and between experiences. This passage is both privileged space and privileged moment, whose "lignes de partage," the boundaries separating place from place, the lines as well of sharing and crossing, are traced in witness to difference and to agreement. Situated at these lines of crossing, poetry resembles and can be understood in its coincidence and coappearance with the other objects in the world; the threshold of sharing (*seuil-partage* or *limen*), which acts also as edge ["lisière"] and as articulating hinge ["charnière"], locates its in-betweenness. Despite its supposed self-referentiality, the poem of the threshold seems for Deguy to swing open freely between words and the world—"Le poème du monde pour le monde du poème" ["the poem of the world for the world of the poem"][4]—as between poet and reader. All passage between is encouraged:

> *Il est besoin d'un lecteur d'un geste d'un papier*
> *D'un miroir Tu es visage ma feuille mon échancrure*
> *Je suis le tissu pour que tu sois ton vide La surface*
> *Pour que froisse la main . . .*
> *Le creux pour ma difficulté le blanc pour que je sois*
> *Ce dessin que je ne serais pas . . .*
>
> A reader a gesture a paper a mirror
> Are needed You are a face my page my opening
> I am the cloth so you may be your void The surface
> For the hand to rumple . . .
> The hollow for my harshness the white so I may be
> This sketch I would not be . . . (OD, 98)

This acknowledged need prevents, as do the self-irony and the frequent revealing mask, a dryness of outlook occasionally threatening in a poet of such rapid turn. Deguy moves all toward an acknowledgment of the profound interior space needed for the inner threshold rather than a purely exterior one: from the *Poèmes de la presqu'île* [*Peninsula Poems*] of 1961, to the massive intellectual landscape of the *Tombeau de Du Bellay* of 1973 the evolution is visible, whereas the more recent travel poems of *Jumelages* and *Made in USA* develop a quite other concept of space as consciousness.

CENTER AND MEETING

> *Le poète aux yeux cernés de*
> *mort descend à ce monde du miracle.*

Que sème-t-il . . . Que favorise-t-il
Aux choses qui n'attendent rien
dans le silence du gris?
la coincidence

The poet with death-circled eyes
comes down to the world of miracle.
What does he sow. . . . What does he privilege
in the things awaiting nothing in the
grey silence?
coincidence

MICHEL DEGUY, *Biefs*

Over the years—for they too form a passage—the origin in an outside center, that "centre au-dehors" from which the landscape was said to emanate (DEP, 7) became the more neutral space of the poem set apart and subsequently of the space as boundary and hinge. The focus then moved inward, the language of poetic questioning acquiring a different stylistic firmness, thereby reaffirming in a new complexity, a sort of theatrical *mise-en-abyme* situated inside, where a scene opens within a scene, like a drawing inside itself, in a new interior that functions as a spatial *halt* within the text. These iterations and inward-spiraling wanderings replace any kernel of referential sense: this is what I would call an *incursive motion*. Of those long exterior wanderings or excursions composing the *Peninsula Poems*, with what Deguy describes as their pauses and their startings, their leavings and returnings, their waiting and their remembering, he composed an order. Afterwards, that order and the questioning of self and of the poem that was first related to the world and then became it passed on to a path less obvious.

And yet, for the reader as for the poet of beginning, "comment dire le centre?" ["How is one to tell the center?" PP, 8]. That interrogation of the "marche," which opened the *Poèmes de la presqu'île*, remains unanswerable.

In 1961 it was a question of boundary: to transpose an inner order to an exterior limit, to set a space apart within another space; the statement of the boundaries overcome is begun by the pairs of contrary terms that already, in their form, signal the implied dialectical structure of the question: "De pierre et de velours, la maison donnait d'habiter le dehors, imminent espace du dedans" ["Of stone and velvet, the house permitted one to live outside, imminent space of the inside," DEP, 78]. This other reversal of perception is the true passage between in and out, where the text is, like the house, the placing of an interior limit on the world outside, the opening-out of the inner space of words on the world, and finally, the creation of the exterior in the interior. The two spaces, hinged by the personal consciousness, are a pair of *comparants*, placed in apposition and *comparution* for the consciousness of coincidence. A continued longing for likeness and situation leads to a reiteration of the same, and a reassembling of the distinct: "Je suis venu pour rassembler" ["I have come to gather," P, 37]. The consciousness of the ephemeral ("the brief here") and value placed on motion lead to the quest of convergence and of meeting place, where distinction and similarity are simultaneously preserved. By one further *acte de naissance*, separate borders become an articulate continuous consciousness. The word acting as border and boundary, as pleat and hinge, as the dramatic spectacle of a language torn apart is, by a fracture, reassembled: "que la rupture rebondisse encore en rencontre" ["let rupture spring up once more in meeting," DEP, 103].

The gap of silence between the linguistic elements leaves room for the advent of some marvel: "There is within the poem, diffused in and between each word, a silence, an interval where the breath is held and meaning also . . . Its *approximation*, its impatience . . . for the approach itself of the poem." (G, 171)

THE POEM OF THE POEM[5]

Ce lieu me suffit

. . .

Pourtant me suffit ce lieu

This place suffices for me

. . .

Still, for me this place suffices
MICHEL DEGUY, *Biefs*

Situated at the crossroads of the opposite movements, observing the reversal of things and signs, the poet *announces* the place and the poem as they write each other. Here is the boundary, as we are clearly told, and the world needs to be announced: "J'écris de ce lieu-ci" ["I write from this place," DEP, 115]. But the sign as hieroglyph, as taken in all its mysterious depth, is rather evocative and interrogative than declamatory: "Quels signes?" ["What signs?" FC, 7]. The passage of one sign into another, as one word passes into another or one figure into its opposite is well illustrated by a swan and sign or "Signe/cygne" present since Mallarmé: "Le cygne dressé/Recommence à parler" ["The swan erect/Begins to speak again"] (OD, 40). In the universe of Deguy, where the inversions are boxed in an inextricable fashion, a *reflection* on passage ("L'inverse et l'inversion de l'inverse/L'enclosent ses reflets et leurs reflets" ["The inverse and inversion of the inverted/Enclose him his reflections and their reflections,"] OD, 53) manages to reflect even on the reflected and to invert the inversion. The surface of the work is doubled by another depth, itself lining or doubling the meditation like another reflection of reflection. "La doublure" puts in play a duplicity of sense, another twinning:

Et ceci la question de la surface
Et du redoublement qui montre
La question du théâtre que le théâtre double

And this question of the surface
And of the redoubling which shows
The question of the theater that the theater
doubles (OD, 100)

And again, the doubling and duplicitous word that serves as lining, or "doublure" also includes the possibility of turning back (as in "doubler") or duplicate a course, and the dubbing of a film, and, further, the passing of another vehicle on a road. Each of these senses contaminates the others and passes into the poem: in these poem-acts, or gestural and dramatic *Actes*, the images flow into each other, and the expressions reflect upon each other.[6]

Similarly, a movement of concentric correspondences seems at one point about to replace the coincidence once recognized. Junctures on the syntactical level as well as the notional level abound; the word "like" and the "comparative genitive" are agents (even double agents) for the objects and ideas playing the principal roles in the theater of language, in their *comparution*, and mutual exposition. Thus acts and beings bordering on each other belong to each other by language and rhetoric. Tropes, masquerades, and even metaphors may lead back to a fresh beginning; the credo consisting of a "MOTION OF CONFIDENCE IN THE GENIUS OF THE LANGUAGE OR PROJECTS OF DISSONANCE" bears sole witness. Thought itself practices its own passing as a *seizure*, but is caught in tapestry, to be rewoven ("retissée") within the text of passage and boundary. Tapestry, theater, festival ("le moment festival du marquage"): the text is again marked as celebratory and presentational. Its dramatic birth needs practice (even in a "concroissante spontanéité"), costume, gesture, and, above all, rehearsal or "repetition." A tireless repetition is said to insert itself in each moment of spectacle, within which the "cipher of origin" can be understood. Each poem repeats the already given echo of words Deguy calls "constitutive," and yet a clear space between words must be reinvented, as it is identical with freedom. Empty space now protects what it alone encloses freely, like the "Figurations" of the poem, which concern equally the portrayal of gesture and of play and the annihilation of inscription: "Writing is in some sense disappearing. . . ." (F, 120) For it is the void that permits the readability of this vestige where things sign their disappearance. The voice is the guardian of the figure traced. In it the outline is sketched (traced and effaced); in it and its "protection" the slightest things *play*, like the dancer ceaselessly imitating exactly *that*: the gesture of effacement or salvation. "Here the spacious illusion intervenes . . . ," (F, 122). Based on Mallarmé's studies of the dancer's movements in their relation to the writing act, this text illustrates, as do the theories of Garelli discussed above, the use of readability for perception and for inscription. Even the negation of readability is set in poetic play.

The void is rendered positive like the fault or fissure in a wall, which permits passage: through such an opening—even in the wall of a tomb, as in the traditional "Tombeau" of Deguy's homage to the Renaissance poet Du Bellay (*Tombeau de Du Bellay*)—the writing figure and the inscribing hand may pass. The figure of the Renaissance poet passes into that of the contemporary one, who in his turn reinserts himself thereby in history; this twin perception of figures, of one text or / and another, is a preview of the twinnings of place in *Jumelages*, like temporal and spatial *double crossings*.[7]

On a final apposition of two texts from the volume of *Jumelages*, called "Comparution," I will rest my case for a poetics of the between as Deguy describes it. The signal one text seems to make toward the other illustrates the expression Deguy takes explicitly from Heidegger, "to wink"; these texts wink at each other. The first concerns the initial rupture from former poetic perception and coding, and the crossroads at which world meets word:

> At the threshold of the pulse of language, the meeting place of a world for the being speaking of it and the poem of a language for a world which matches its figure, in this sharing, stands a *subject* as in the utopia finding its metaphor in every border: the scene of the pleat, of the difference of the world in its figurants, as of the place where the wood *breaks off* with the field, the ocean with the earth. (J, 28)[8]

It is on this threshold that the intricate exchange between language and life, of the text as of the world, speaker and reader, takes place. "Language 'plays' like any articulation, groove . . . limping, groping, equivocal, biased, obliqueness, intransitivity: *the parts of the symbol never adapt themselves*. Integrally, the articulation ("brisure") is marked, even 'stuck together again . . . '. The symbol is the fault, the groove, the articulation, the loss, through which meaning escapes . . ." (J, 160). Loss and recuperation, like the effacement and salvation of the figure, form the articulate hinge of the work of writing and of reading. Here meaning is always approximate and interchange is always to be re-examined, in the open play of the passage of the poem.

JACQUES DUPIN
Inscription on the Rise

Vigiles sur le promontoire. Ne pas descendre. Ne plus se taire.
Vigils on the lookout point. Not to go down. No longer to be silent.

JACQUES DUPIN, *L'Embrasure*[1]

The passage mapped out in this last reading is presented as an arduous uphill climb: a *Gravir* in act as in the title Dupin has given to one of his major works. The difficulty of the ascent is equated with that of writing. His language will stress increasingly a rupture of syntax, sound, and rhetoric, a willed loss and degradation undertaken to discover the integral wholeness of a world "poetically sayable and sharable," a willed blindness as the necessary prelude to vision. This movement between two acts held paradoxically together is characteristic of all four poets in this last section, each with different elements to oppose and link. Dupin balances negativity, opacity, and contraction on one hand, and dissemination, resurgence, and imagination on the other. Images corresponding to these attitudes are recognizable throughout his writings, and their melodramatic opposition jars at first with the extreme understatement detectable on a second reading. I will not attempt to treat the problem of Dupin's own irony, suggested in this displacement. It is as much a problem of reading as of writing, and gives to both their challenge in this case—of a special and highly complex sensibility, covered over by the modesty of a poet who chooses not to impose himself as poet.

Dupin's earliest poems, in *Cendrier du voyage* [*Ashtray of Travel*, 1950] included in *Gravir*, 1963, already indicate a motion whose consumption and consummation are simultaneously implied within the title, as the paradoxical difficulty remains in the text and its defeat. From here to the upward climb of *Gravir* and the evident reticence of attitude apparent in such a title as his *Embrasure*, that recess of a window or a wall, that nichelike insert even within a mountain, all the metaphoric steps compose a passage at once made and consumed, revealed and withdrawn, stamped and engraved upon the memory, whose trace is more inset than evident: an inscription at once inside as, as in a yet later title, outside: *Dehors*.

A LANGUAGE BUILT IN BREAKING

Migrations incessantes des mots jusqu'au dernier à travers l'écriture, tentative pour rendre un seul instant visible à leur crête celui qui disparaît déjà . . . quelque chose d'édifié et de rompu . . .

Incessant migrations of words down to the last, through writing, an attempt to show for one moment on their crest the one already disappearing . . . something edified and broken . . .

JACQUES DUPIN, *Gravir*

Writing as rupture commences the construction of an edifice by destroying it. "Commencer comme on déchire un drap, le drap dans les plis duquel on se regardait dormir" ["To begin as you tear a sheet, the sheet in whose folds you saw yourself sleeping," G, 76]. The distance from an earlier attitude is clearly marked: when the hero-poet in Breton's poem "Vigilance" sets fire to the sheets where he sees his double sleeping, it is with an intention toward an eventual and available wholeness, for whose labyrinthean depths he keeps Ariadne's thread: "Je tiens le fil." The optimism of the surrealists' "champs magnétiques" or magnetic fields is gravely altered in Dupin's "champs fragmentaires," those partial fields echoing with a possibility of song, those "chants" of a fragment. An alchemical resource of transmutation by fire still pervades the poetic scene, although the act, however violent, is a simple revolutionary gesture against a formerly passive state and vision.

The nonpassive character is reflected in the two sets of poems collected in *Gravir*: "Les Brisants" ["The Breakers" of 1958] and "Saccades" ["Jolts" of 1962], the term "Brisants" suggesting also, by extension, the word "brisées," like traces left or inscribed, and "Gravir" suggesting the vertical task of the poet, climbing, and by phonetic extension that of engraving ("graver"), as if the word were to be inscribed deeply, while at a level ever higher, having both plunge and rise.[2] *L'Embrasure* (1969) stands in relation to that task as a niche set into the mountain. In *Gravir*, "Les Lichens" mark the way along an upward path, addressing directly the mountain of poetry:

Te gravir et, t'ayant gravie—quand la lumière ne prend plus appui sur les mots, et croule et dévale—te gravir encore.

To climb you and, having climbed you—when the light no longer leans on words, and crumbles and plunges down—to climb you once more.

(G, 70)[3]

This passage with its clear erotic tinge, is built on convergence and suppression, for the word on which one leans is also, by a minor addition, the mountain climbed: *mot/mont.*

The path traveled by the poet toward the line of conscious rupture is named, with signposts or titles indicating the way: The *Moraines* are the signs of glacier rock, the convex contrary of the circuses dug out by the glacial force. The latter "arènes" can also be seen as recessed "embrasures," the term implying also, by phonetic suggestion "embraser" or the *burning* of the word, this ignition being the process dialectically opposed to the icy advance of nature. The punctuation is read upon the page of the mountainside:

Pour la distribution de nouveaux signes, au-delà, sans la piste d'un texte ou le sillage d'une voix gelée. Le Jeu découvre et recouvre leurs traces ponctuelles. Leurs ombres transparentes se multiplient, se croisent, délimitent une aire,—arène, échiquier, page blanche—, que leur absence physique illumine.

For the distribution of new signs, beyond, with neither the slope of a text nor the furrow of a frozen voice. The Game discovers and recovers their punctual traces. Their transparent shadows multiply, cross one another, stake out a domain—arena, chess board, white page—, illuminated by their actual absence.

(E, 72)

So the "arène" is the replacement of Mallarmé's page as the ground staked out for conflict, a dangerous space set apart, where the game of poetry is played.

The thrust toward a gravity of language, toward an inscription made profound, extends to a meditation on the weight of all signs, of objects emptied of what they once contained, stripped of their exterior vestments:

> *La lampe éteinte est-elle plus légère?*
> Is the extinguished lamp lighter?

and elsewhere:

> *Plus lourde d'être nue*
> Heavier for being naked

Although the rhythm of the first quotation is reminiscent of Eluard's interrogation used as a title in a collection of 1951: "*La jarre peut-elle être plus belle que l'eau?*" [Can the container be any lovelier than the water?"], the sense is reversed and complicated in its correspondence with the second. Dupin's inscriptions, crisscrossed, retrace one another.

The tension, insofar as all relations in this poetry can be said to be examples of tension, voltage, or stress—that is, between the break and the breaking, the split and the split apart, the crevice and the trace—forms a complex canvas stretched out of the poem and of its self-examining. The investigation and the confession probe into the texture of the work, with a cutting motion fatal to the substance of the word, like an inexorable incision. The two currents of break and trace are joined, the latter made possible only by a destruction of the surface: a moving sleep or a wakefulness "shattering its support" ("Qui pulvérise ce qui la supporte," E, 61), inflicting, necessarily, fissures and gaps. This matter and this form are to be undone, by themselves alone.

The text entitled "Le Présent d'une nuit" further exemplifies this metatextual concern, to which it supplies a specific parallel:

> *Ce roc assailli d'étoiles, aux crevasses duquel la lèpre, avant l'éloge, avait progressé sans mesure, allait-il se soumettre à la paresseuse cadence de la source des morts? Le bal était défait, les danseurs transparents. Le sang coula, l'herbe devint profonde. A l'aube, en grand secret, les lèvres des amants heurtèrent une rosée illimitée.*

This rock assailed by stars, whose crevices had flaked away immeasurably before the time of praise, was it going to give in to the lazy rhythm of the fall of deadmen's springs? The dance was undone, the dancers made transparent. Blood flowed, grass deepened. At dawn, in profound secret, the lovers' lips grazed an unlimited dew. (G, 41)

The harsh assault of the initial image suggests the upward struggle, the heights assaulted, whre the morains and circuses left by the glacier make irreversible marks upon the canvas ("*étoile*"). This text is deeply inscribed or de-scribed, engraved by crevices and yet standing in relief by its morains ("as*saillie*"): its own heights must be read against those deep crevices, each one echoing the other. As the morain disrupts the mountain profile by an irregular addition, so the flaking away of the circuses, as by a malady ("la lèpre" read in its literal sense) makes an irregular subtraction and destruction in the matter already assailed. Now, by the substitution of one letter, phonetically close, the lips of the poet speaking attack the ground of the text. The incisive *gravity* of the poetic word makes a deliberate wound: on the page, or the canvas, or here, on the grass, this incision serves as the central source for the text, flowing with the ink of blood, as in the expression "l'encre coula," which here becomes: "le sang coula."

La lèpre → [la lèvre] → les lèvres des amants

Profundity is thus conferred upon the matter *engraved* ("l'herbe devint profonde") "grass deepened," as the wound reveals its positive aspect, the word "gravir" implying an upward movement always to be seen alongside the engraving with which it is paradoxically associated, as in the phonetically similar word, "graver." Furthermore, the color of the blood suggests, by a visual-aural transfer, the rose of dawn:

une rosée illimitée → [une rose est illimitée]

This implied redness of the lips, that is, of the dancers, and of the lovers whom they figure, echoing in its turn the transformation "lèpre"—"lèvres," so that the malady is built into the speaking and the dance, acts self-signaling and self-condemning. Still along that ambiguously traced line, the rhythm of the dance ("mesure") and its beat is again implied:

soumettre → [mètre]

suggesting the term of undoing: "défait."

For, in fact, this text, like the others that resemble it, unravels itself in its construction; the consciousness of time's fatality ("nuit, présent, heure") and the phonetic echo of the hour:

heure → [heurt]

is never absent from this space unceasingly destroyed. In such a dark setting, the "nuit" of the title can also be read as an intimate danger, the harm done by time ("heures") or the jolts of language ("heurts") to the moment of the text and to its innate rhythm:

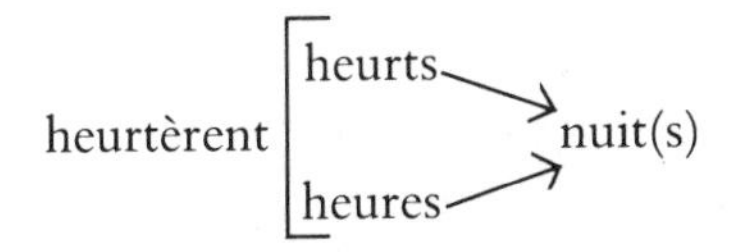

Finally, the gesture will force a silence, when the dancers will lose their step and their power of speech:

"–tèrent" =
"lèvres" → [taire]

Thus the *excess of writing* ["le mouvement excessif," E, 61] declared here to be "without measure" or "unlimited," can plunge again toward its suicide, which is also the source of its earthy strength, and the guarantee of its lasting fascination as a text.

LINKINGS

Paroles, alluvions régressives . . .
Words, regressive alluvia . . .
JACQUES DUPIN, *L'Embrasure*

Moraines, metapoetical and self-reflexive, commences with an interrogation about writing itself, to which no one answer can be given: "Écrire, est-ce . . . ?" The first poem is dominated by its opposite, and by the image of an eye wide-open—our own invisibility inflicted on us by our words—and leads into the other poems, where again sight and text are inextricably interwoven.

The investigation thus turns about a vision first crazed, "cet oeil effaré" and "sa pupille envenimée," a frightened eye and its envenomed pupil, and then reversed; for the writer at the center of vision is denied by his very sight:

Comme si j'étais condamné à voir en marchant. En parlant. A voir ce dont je parle et à parler justement parce que je ne vois pas. Donc à donner à voir ce que je ne vois pas, ce qu'il m'est interdit de voir.

As if I were condemned to see while walking. While speaking. To see what I am speaking of and to speak precisely because I see nothing. Thus, to present to sight what I do not see, what I am forbidden to see. (E, 69)

To see is almost always to read in this universe of metatext, where the trap of the word marked out and yet devoid of its name functions as a gigantic book, empty and therefore imprisoning the writer, who breathes in only the air of his own limitless labyrinth. Like a prison always prepared, the reader's open eye meets that of the poet or of the text. The only element constant here is distance: the writer is separated from his seeing as from the object aimed at by his words, which he is said to desire, and he is incorporated in that distance. From his encounter with the object in a sudden lifting of that prohibition, a space bounds forth into the open, like the violent bursting apart of a seed, murderous to the shell. "Un espace jaillit . . . ." Thus the writer is the murderer of his object, which is his subject, and the innocent slaughterer of himself, together with his text:

visage lié à la répétition
d'un meurtre

face linked to a repetition
to a murder (EG, 203)

The seeing and the writing and reading are taken to be the instruments of future suicide, in a blind and perfect aim, the faultless vision of a distance that one moment drastically denies, as the bullet leaves the gun, the latter here marked by the statement of its absence: "nul fusil." In a passage of this rigor, such an overt ellipse of weapon gives all the greater play to the implicit drama. Not only is it the case that what is said is not present, but that the single word heard most loudly in these texts is thundered forth at last, as a tardy and affirmative answer to a question not even posed:

Le "oui" longtemps réprimé comme si son retard devait augmenter la charge, accroître l'ampleur de l'explosion et rendre irréversible le départ. Il tonne.

The "yes" long repressed as if its delay was to increase its charge, increasing the force of the explosion and making the departure irreversible. It resounds. (E, 63)

Yet this response, which is a positive deployment of mental energy, attains in the long run nothing more than an essential emptiness: "Car l'écriture ne nous rend rien. La consumation même est imparfaite" ["For writing gives us nothing in return. Consummation itself is imperfect," E, 63].

Poem after poem has at its basis this rhythm of an action carried out, declared in no uncertain terms, and subsequently negated, as the annihilating power is seen to deepen our torment and to clench the fatal association between language and life. The poet, perceiving that the descent to the abyss will be simultaneous with the upward striving of *Gravir*, walks forward with a certain step to his own destruction. If he claims birth from the knot of events ("le noeud dont je naissais" EMB, 64) he claims it equally, by phonetic implication, from the beginning of the invited negation, as if it were to read: / "le (ne) dont je naissais" ["the nothing from which I was born."] Such a double reading, based on a negative force implicit for the ear in the apparently simple image of the knot, recalls similar occurrences, such as two claustrophobic examples of strangulation: "Le noeud d'asphyxie formelle" ["The knot of formal asphyxia" G, 19] and "Etranglé dans chaque noeud de mon poème" ["Strangled in each knot of my poem," G, 28]. Coming to physical or linguistic life requires a most difficult passage: "J'ai cru traverser vivant, les yeux ouverts, le noeud dont je naissais. . . . Je l'ai cru" ["I thought I crossed while living, my eyes open, the knot from which I was born . . . I believed it," E, 64].

The potency of this poetry lives chiefly in the renewal of this traversal of a psychological abyss, in the accentuation of its rhythm repeated throughout the work; the latter denies its own transcendence, conscious that words abuse us, in their projection and their ambivalent negativity, the underlying condition for birth as writing.

INTERVAL, GAP

In place of the constant or unbroken images of an earlier imagination stands the discontinuous chain of this poetry: images such as the broken wall, the torn leaf, the fissured language, the breach in being, mark the place of the lacunae sensible in our statements, poetic or prosaic. The light breaking over contemporary poetry shatters what it touches, and is itself intermittent, as is the object it reveals. Dupin's "livre intermittent" (G, 78) responds to our discontinuous and deconstructed reading, as the interruption of the sign or of its tracks reflects upon us and our system of signs, based on difference for comprehension: "L'écart qui nous recommence" ["The difference that begins us again," EG, 204]. The expression of a pulsation or beat (as in "the beat of my sentence"), recurring frequently, signals exactly this coming and going, this impulse responding to the divergent rays of the wounded light thrown upon it in uneven patches like the long and short patterning of the following text countered on a linguistic pulsation:

Malgré l'étoile fraîchement meurtrie
qui bifurque
—c'est sa seule cruauté le battement
de ma phrase qui s'obscurcit
et se dénoue—

Despite the star freshly bruised
dividing in two

—its only cruelty the beating
of my sentence darkening
and unknotting— (E, 53)

"La Nuit grandissante" ["The Increasing Night"], the title of the series from which the quotation above is taken, is an examination of this intervalent light, as its "bifurcated passion" is metaphorically split apart on the anvil of the poem. The light is itself the mountain against which the text is engraved, the murderous slope where a harsh and difficult breathing is heard. Troubled, the beat, although by the poet's own confession powerful and fecund, remains ambivalent: if at moments a verbal opacity is seen as opening to the light, at other moments it opens only on a word laden with shadow ("chargé d'ombre"). The alternation of ambivalence: shadow/shadow, light/shadow, or shadow/light provides the energy that relies on interval, difference, unequal intensity. "Mobilité du poème qui ne cesse d'entrecroiser les fils tendus et d'en déchirer le tissage pour ouvrir le corps à un afflux d'obscurité" ["Mobility of the poem which never ceases to crisscross the threads stretched out or to rend the fabric, opening the body to a rush of darkness," EP, 456].

In contrary correspondence with "La Nuit grandissante," Dupin's prose poem "Le Soleil substitué" ["The Substituted Sun"], in the last issue of the deliberately ephemeral journal *L'Ephémère* (no. 20), examines not an intermittent nocturnal light but the radiance of an invisible writing, the missing *texte* suggesting, by the drop of one letter, the image of a *tête*, like the circle of the sun behind a blackboard, as if the paradoxical dark brilliance of the baroque were to be perceived just behind a horizon on which there remained several traces of other texts. The movement begins with an effacement on that horizon, as a "cloudy" cloth glides over a blackboard's obscurity, cloudy with the misty white chalk of a nocturnal inscription, previously erased. "Qu'est-ce qui reste que la main peut toucher?" ["What remains for the hand to touch?" EP, 450] demands the poet.

There remains only what is outside: "hors du tableau," beyond the blackboard, or the canvas that might open at any moment as its matter is ripped ("matérialité déchireé"). Fear is all-pervading, that such a passage might be made within us and yet, suddenly, not within us, fear of opening onto a non-sense:

Nous sommes le non-lieu et le non-objet d'une gravitation de signes insensés. . . . Nous sommes le non-lieu et le non-objet de leur élan destructeur, le champs dévasté de leur conjonction et de leur divergence. Gisement à ciel ouvert.

We are the non-place and the non-object of a gravitation of senseless signs. We are the non-place and the non-object of their destructive thrust, the devastated field of their conjunction and their divergence. Vein exposed to the sky.
(EP, 452)

The sun or the text its substitute, in the intervalence of its illumination, detaches itself from us, and in so doing, displaces the threshold of readability ("le seuil de la lisibilité," EP, 455). *Seuil/soleil* or *texte/tête*: the echoes are themselves repetitions and displacements, phonetic slidings, the resounding difference from which the poem is made and from which it takes its sparse matter. But finally, in the process of decapitation, that recurrent and traditional slaughter to which the "cou coupé" or severed neck of Apollinaire's "Zone" also refers, the sun remains as metaphor and resplendent replacement, the present substitute for the text that stood at its head: "Il s'avance au devant du texte comme sa pierre d'achoppement de rupture, et la brèche où se rafraîchit le rayon d'une tête absente" ["It advances before the text as its stumbling block, its source of rupture, and the breach where the rays of an absent head are refreshed," EP, 458].

The radiant passage ends on the writing with which *Moraines* began: "Ecrire," like an infinitive of openness, uninflected. In this case there is no reopening of the question ("écrire, est-ce . . . ?"), but rather a response as violent as the text is violent, as the blackboard changes to its opposite, as mirror of the murderous interval: "notre sang pour tain de ce miroir: *écrire*" ["our blood for this mirror's silvering: *writing*" EP, 459]. But the mirror spins around, like a spectacle "moaning on its axis." A more complicated reflection is then made upon the whole question of traversal, collective as the *tableau* is exposed, and individual, as the reader's measure is taken by the text: "la traversée qui nous scande, la trajectoire qui nous mesure" ["the traversal scanning us, the trajectory measuring us," EG, 190].

SIGN, TRACE

For a topographical passage to be formed, a difference must be marked, visible or sensible or audible against a neutral surface. A form or line or instant suffices, discovered by accident or hollowed out on purpose: "une ligne nous absout" ["a line absolves us," E, 110]. Among the procedures by which Dupin inscribes a difference, three in particular hold our interest: each relies on an ambiguous source and a fragmentary but distinctive vision, briefly expressed: "l'inintelligible fragment, / Que ne trahit que sa couleur imprécatoire" ["The unintelligible fragment, / Betrayed only by its imprecating color," G, 58].

Disproportion

The reader's potential sensitivity to disproportion is akin to and developed by the sensitivity to the dislocation and the setting awry of collective and individual experience. Stress may be laid on the small perception as a path to the larger one, like a reflection in the text of the *way* of perceiving and its vitalization of the surrounding space, made personal:

Par une brèche dans le mur,
La rosée d'une seule branche
Me rendra tout l'espace vivant . . .

Through a gap in the wall,
The dew of a single branch
Will render all space living for me . . .
(G, 56)

As, for example, the smoke of a fisherman's fire pierces the monotonous completion of an "absolute horizon," so the poetic protrusions are noticeable despite their insertion into a continuous background, but they must, upon occasion, be pointed to in order to be perceived. In a poem whose title sets it in the mode of description of an exterior scene, "Le Paysage" ["The Landscape"], this conclusion follows directly upon an incomplete sentence, interrupted to force the attention on this specific moment: "Par quelle aberration de perspective suis-je encore attentif à la persévérance d'un chardon sur le talus d'en face?" ["By what aberration of perspective am I still aware of the thistle persevering on the slope across from me?", G, 45]. The interrogation magnifies the details and their degree of distinction, as if certain differences formerly grasped in high relief were now to have been moved to a field of bas-relief. Dupin's care in singling out this change of perspective as an aberration determines our perception of it as just that. In the series "La Proximité du murmure" ["Nearness of the Murmur"], we are able to read the suppression of the writing subject as revealing the sufficient bareness of the text itself against the extraordinary shadowed background of excess, enlivening or vitalizing a prior neutrality, as in the first example of the branch and space:

J'ai négligé son dénuement
elle se tient un peu plus haut
ombre démesurée d'une roue de charrette
sur le mur lourdement vivant

I have neglected its bareness
it is found a little higher
excessive shadow of a cart wheel
on the wall awkwardly alive

(E, 28)

As a preface for the text "L'Onglée" and as a further example of the disproportionality used to vitalize both perception and setting, we might observe the smallest space of the fingernail, which is seen as sufficient to contain the reflection of an entire scene (as the nail is potentially the writing hand):

Là, le simulacre d'un grand feu inclina ses reflets sur mon ongle. Cette absence de sens et de vues, je m'engouffrai dans son manteau de roi.

There the semblance of a great fire threw its reflections on my fingernail. This absence of sense and of views, I was swallowed up within its kingly cloak. (G, 40)

The most modest outgrowth of the body may serve as hearth for the flames cast on a novel perception. In the same text, a further display of the potency of this tiny part of the hand complements the invisible force of the wind by the opposition of its tranquil, obvious, and minute surface. "Mon amour, le vent n'était pas plus rapide au milieu de la mer qu'à la surface de ton ongle" ["My love, the wind was no more rapid at the center of the sea than over your fingernail's surface," G, 81]. These minor tracings of "L'Onglée" leave the mark of this powerful nail, like the minimal groove of a sign of writing scratched with a force out of all proportion to its actual space.

Repetition

Slightly altered or identical, lines doubled or folded over on themselves form a *re-pli* like a repeat and a re-pleat, exemplified by two passages in *Lichens*:

Même si la montagne se consume, même si les survivants s'entretuent. . . . Sur le versant clair paissent nos troupeaux. Sur le versant abrupt paissent nos troupeaux.

Even if the mountain consumes itself, even if the survivors kill one another. . . . On the bright slope graze our flocks. On the abrupt slope graze our flocks. (G, 63)

The placid sound of the words "paissent" and "troupeaux," whose phonetic suggestion of "paix" and "eau" ("peace" and "water"), contrasts vividly with the conceptual violence of the two preceding verbs "se consume" and "s'entretuent," together with the dual force of the sharp adjectives in "versant clair" and "versant abrupt," to form a balance in which the text gathers its rhythmic strength at the outset. The first sentence in its double beginning is suspended rather than closed by the punctuation (. . . .), and its continuation in the second doublet gives a half-response to the implicit question "what if . . . ?" The continuity of form reflects a continuity of feeling: "in any case . . ." or "even so. . . ." Even in the apparent exteriority of the description of mountain and sheep, in the pattern of this echoing construction the way is prepared for a profoundly interior interweaving of personal statements theoretical and emotional, couched in the same repetitive form: "Ce que je vois et que je tais m'épouvante. Ce dont je parle, et que j'ignore, me délivre. Ne me délivre pas." ["What I see and keep silent appalls me. What I speak of and what I am unaware of frees me. Does not free me," G, 65].

The ambiguous but deliberate balance here marks a second step up the mountain seen as an elementary, monumental unity: "On vous a trompés. La lumière est simple. Et les collines proches" ["You have been deceived. The light is simple. And the hills near," G, 69]. The odd psychological density of this quite simple statement is felt against the inner formal complexity of the mental progress up the mountain of writing, justifying the slow ascent of poet and reader alike: "Te gravir et, t'ayant gravie . . . te gravir encore" (G, 70). Along this narrow path, all the links of having and holding, of suffering and joy, are finally denied: "Ni possession, ni passion" (G, 71).

On the other hand, the pattern of repetition used as ending can reassure after a period of interrogation or suspension or ardent ascent. For example, in a poem where ocean and mountain render their drowned and their dead, a correspondence is made clear with the observing and narrating mind, in the double exception that closes the poem:

Et leurs ailes jonchent la mer. Leurs ailes, leurs griefs: nos impatiences déroutées. . . . Je ne sais rien de nous, excepté peut-être ce rivage qui s'éloigne dans le matin, excepté cette barque qui n'a pas sombré.

And their wings litter the sea. Their wings, their grievances: our impatiences led astray. . . . I know nothing of us, except perhaps this shore growing distant in the morning, except this boat which has not foundered. (G, 81)

Despite its questioning, the poem does not sink or hesitate. These texts, "unreadable," as the poet calls them, profound in tone and substance, take their beginning in the celebrated injunction to destruction and self-destruction, perfectly ruptured:

Commencer comme on déchire un drap . . . l'acte d'écrire comme rupture . . . dans une succession nécessaire de ruptures, de dérives, d'embrasements.

To begin as you tear a sheet . . . the act of writing as rupture . . . in a necessary succession of ruptures, of deflections, of blazes. (E, 76)

The extreme sensitivity responsible for that text is instantly evident in the following one, balanced between nature and culture, forest and stars, night and field, book and hearth, work and game:

La forêt nous tient captifs. Et le nombre. Et la solitude. . . . En haut, le livre ruisselant. En bas, nos amours pétrifiés, avec le cérémonial de la peste. Entre eux . . . l'échancrure du jeu.

Etre, n'avoir rien. Il suffit qu'ils soient: astres, foyers de raison sans mesure. Qu'ils fonctionnent ici, dans la nuit battante, l'indifférence, à proximité de nos murs. Et que leur énergie, par instants, les renverse. Nous disloque. Irrigue nos traces. Irrigue nos champs fragmentaires.

The forest holds us captive. And number. And solitude. . . . Above, the streaming book. Below, our loves petrified, with the ceremonial of the plague. Between them . . . the indentation of the game.

Being, having nothing. It is enough for them to be: stars, hearths of immeasurable reason. For them to function here, in the beating night, in indifference, near our walls. And for their energy, at moments, to overturn them. Disjointing us. Watering our tracks. Irrigating our fragmentary fields. (E, 93)

Read on the simplest metatextual level the poem holds us in its typographical forest, like the open trap already glimpsed. The book is a ritual sacrifice where the violence of the linguistic game is worked out and openly declared. Constellations of words dislocate ordinary reason, leaving senseless tracks and disconnected utterances, whose fragmented discourse is heard here. The sustained reading of the ambivalence, "chants" along with "champs," permits the simultaneous suggestion of the word and of the field cultivated through the text. Compare, in *Gravir*, "le chant qui est de soi-même sa faux" ["the song which is its own scythe," G, 56].

As for the device of repetition, the statement in triadic form: "la forêt . . . le nombre. Et la solitude," is echoed by the triple directions: "En haut. . . . En bas. . . . Entre eux . . . ." Prepared by these patterns, the final paragraph is saturated with repetitions that assume an unusual force: "il suffit qu'ils . . . qu'ils . . ." and that make an abbreviated formal echo. "Nous disloque. . . . Irrigue. . . . Irrigue . . ."; the paragraph itself thus becomes the third member of a greater triadic form, like a repetitive set in a set, and so on. Finally, the dry beginning leads like an epic forest, through the ceremony and the game to the imploration of an end to dryness and to the Waste Land, its own verbal flow serving to irrigate the traces of a language dry and dislocated, as in the verb "renverse"or "to pour," itself containing also the *verse* ("vers"). In its turn, this verb leads us by phonetic recall back to the verb *s'inverser*, the key to an earlier statement in the same series about the intensification of conciousness and the possibility of *traversal* like a basic change of sign, within the passage made by poet and reader together, constructed:

> *Mais sa violence, sa faiblesse et son incohérence ont pouvoir de s'inverser dans l'opération poétique et, par un retournement fondamental, qui le consume sans le grandir, de renouveler le pacte fragile qui maintient l'homme ouvert dans sa division, et lui rend le monde habitable.*
>
> But its violence, its weakness and its incoherence have the power of inversion in the poetic operation, and, in a basic reversal, which consumes without aggrandizing, to renew the fragile pact which keeps man open in his division and makes the world livable for him. (E, 65)

The fragile pact between reader and text permits the development of such a sensitivity to repeated sounds, enables a re-reading of just such marked passages.

Suppression

An opposite device characteristic of these texts is an elimination or ellipsis of the central link, when the subject is strongly felt or expected because of the contextual framework. The two following examples are both centered on the subject of writing and still focused around the defining interrogation: "Ecrire, est-ce . . . ?" The first is taken from the opening of the collection *L'Embrasure* and, moreover, from the brief liminal poem appropriately called a short cut, "Le Raccourci": "J'écrirai comme elle jaillit, / Vertigineuse, gutturale . . ." ["I shall write as it surges forth, / Vertiginous, guttural . . . ," E, 9]. Here the word *writing* is suppressed in the harshness of the text, set against a backdrop of difficulty; this passage should be balanced against two others within "L'Onglée," the entire text already set numerically backward (7–6–5) into the end of a volume of collected works. They form the end of the collection (1–0) reading backwards, or its opening in reverse, if read from the inside. In the complication of this sort of reversed passage, the past may be read behind the future, a procedure seen in the lines: "J'extrais de demain / l'oubli persistant d'une rose aujourd'hui" ["I extract from tomorrow / the persistent forgetting of today's rose," E, 26] or again the image of the trees perhaps to be cut down: "les stères de bois en puissance." The texts are here to be read in parallel:

1

. . .

mais la table sur laquelle ton corps *se casse*
est de pierre, est immense *est torride*
est battue *par un vent qui ne faiblit pas*

0

. . .

Elle *son corps imprononçable*

comme une amande qu'on brise
entre deux pierres *disparues*

1

but the table on which your body is broken
is of stone, immense torrid
is beaten by a wind which keeps its force

0

She her unpronounceable body

like an almond one breaks open
between two stones disappeared (EG, 208–9)

One of the possible links suppressed for this ellipsis is the suggestion of ambivalence "amande / amante" (lover and almond). In *La Nuit grandissante*, the following lines have a semantic richness of the same type as above, composed of the possible figures of poetry, fruit, and love united in the term "amande." This suggested unity is then put in balance with the opposition fire / frigidity and the repetition "elle se doit / elle se donne." These three differing techniques (assimilation and ambivalence, contrast, and echo) make an arresting texture for the enigmatic appearance of the almond and the love affair, of whatever sort it may be: "Entre la diane du poème et son tarissement / . . . / elle jaillit, l'amande du feu. . . . comme elle se doit elle se donne / et brûle / avec de froides précautions" ["Between the reveille of the poem and its silence / there surges forth the almond of fire / . . . as she must she gives herself, burning / with cold precautions," E, 57]. In these two examples of writing as corporeal,—the body of writing, the link with the primitive is evident: a stone table serves for the brutal maiming of the body (and the body of poetry) in the most extreme of gestures, a sacrificial altar or a writing desk on which the ardent body is broken by the raging wind of the word. "Lui, le scribe accroupi . . ." ["he, the scribe squatting"]. Adopting the primitive and ritual attitude, the poet and scribe kills his object without naming it, like an annihilating gesture of possession and passion.[4] The illumination cast into the passage by this gesture has the same quality as Breton's beauty; it will be convulsive, or it will not be.

A REFLECTIVE PASSAGE

C'est la peau du dehors qui se retourne et nous absorbe

It's the skin of the outside which turns back and absorbs us

JACQUES DUPIN, *Dehors*

After the complex violence of the preceding volume, *Dehors* initiates, already in its title, a question of ambiguous reading, for the poem turning inside out, drawing us out or in, has the flexibility of a Moebius strip, where the interior and the exterior seem to converge along the same line. More than the earlier works of Dupin those in the volume *Dehors* serve as a mirroring device for the observer's gaze, simultaneously, a reflection and a deflection.

The initial poem, "La Ligne de rupture" ["The Line of Rupture"], shows a division as in a mirror image whose doubling device is formally triumphant over the solitude of the speaker. Might we read "Dehors" as an imperative "Out!" hurled against the reader, once trapped by the text and now banished from it? That rupture would be grave, and its line, a perilous high wire; the linear images continue throughout and signal the only partly figurative danger reading entails, as delicate as any fine cut. When the metaphoric line is minimized into a simple shoelace, or the scratch of a single nail only, a streak or a trace—*ligne, lacet, onglée, trait*—a slight irony at the minimalization adds to the discomfort.

The majority of the poems commence with violence in act or thought: verbs of collapse in "La Ligne de rupture," and of effacement in "Le Soleil substitué," are juxtaposed with descriptions of oppression and torture, complete with anvil and pincers and acid heated to the boiling point ("Sang"), of trepanning ("L'Onglée"), of bleeding and expectoration ("Chapurlat"). A "meticulous" disaster ("Trait pour trait")—as delicate as the line itself—is followed by examples of betrayal, of expulsion, dissolution and withering ("Un récit") and of catastrophe ("Ou meurtres"). A plethora of signs seen as "macerated" ("Pour une cassure de fond") produces a slippage of planes and induces verbs of piercing and spurting, in a long poem dedicated to the painter Kasimir Malevitch. Three characteristics are sensed throughout the entire volume: reflection, aggression, and intensity, in a complicated relation to each other. The very thinness of the scratch compresses such action as there is into the smallest of possible spaces, maximizing the feeling of aggression, which reflects upon itself in its repetitions and mirroring; the compression and intensity are suffocating, so that the impulse of the reader may well be directed toward an escape outside, *Dehors*. Nevertheless, this series of negative images, all concerned with the act of writing, is reflected on—and as mirror images *change the sign* and reverse the signal—is finally transformed from negative to positive in this volume of poetry, in which the images are constantly reflected and contained. The reader can only read and then write in turn, upon this minimal and suffocating surface of reflection, by turns smoothly and harshly catastrophic.

This final reading, then, takes place in a reflective passage, "dans l'espace retourné comme une glace vide véridique" ["in the space reversed like an empty veracious mirror," D, 15]. The formal and psychological traces of a subtle version of mirror writing are left everywhere in the inverse formations along the "line of rupture":

> *La traversée qui nous scande, la trajectoire qui nous mesure*
>
> . . .
>
> *nous, la mesure de la traversée, la scansion de la trajectoire*
>
> The traversal scanning us, the trajectory measuring us
>
> . . .
>
> we, the traversal's measure, the trajectory's scansion
>
> (D, 140)

Here the traversal and the trajectory, the scansion and the measure, are all self-contained references to the writing as it reflects upon itself, like twin anguished hostages to the desire of the poet reflecting on the text at once created and stifled by the intensity of the reflection. Even in the phonetic structure, the mirroring is evident: "la lame" (D, 20). The images themselves are often established in systematic balance of opposites. For example, the red of blood is seen against the gleaming white of linen, announced by the thin blade of a guillotine whetted like a razor, working to separate reflection from reflection: "au couperet de toute balance les éclats du linge et le sang contradictoire" ["at the cutting edge of every scale the flashes of linen and the contradictory blood," D, 10]. As the initial image of the skin outside recurs to cover the volcano, containing the fire of "indivision" after the initial scattering of signs, all the possible terror of writing appears metaphorically, as the text breaks open under the force of the explosive future; the volcano erupts, leaving the merged person of victim, poet, and reader with a bloodied mouth, walking upon white ashes from which even the ocean has retreated. Thus each of us is victimized as we read, write, or desire to write. The "glace vide véridique" ("empty veracious mirror") is mirrored in the emptiness of a windowpane, wherein "la vitre est le vide," and the reflection sets the oppositions in play.

The density of Dupin's poetic prose and the intense radiation from its violent source set it apart from the calmer and less intense meditations of many other contemporary poets, although "Le Soleil substitué" stands in correspondence with Ponge's "Le Soleil mis-en-abyme" ["The Sun Set in Death"] and "Sang" ["Blood"] has traces of Apollinaire's "cou coupé," in its livid crimson and its phonetic reflection. The double hostage from the initial text has prepared the doubled sun in the present one, as the sun is itself a double of the fire and the blood at the outset: "Mais la ligne de partage est acérée, ligne double, esclave et maîtresse, relief et gravure" ["But the line of division is steel-sharp, a double line, slave and mistress, relief and engraving," EP, 457]. We are, reader and poet, the ones sacrificed here, in the mirror, the border of which the sharing and dividing line, this "ligne de partage," has already demarcated: "notre sang pour tain de ce miroir: *écrire*" ["our blood as the silvering of this mirror: to write," D, 100].

The title "Sang" ("Blood") includes all the images of fire, sun, and bleeding sacrifice within itself, the sign forcing its attention upon us; that *signe* is also a double of the *sang*, as a table streaming with blood (D, 39) first indicates clearly. Once the connection is established, the reading functions in the manner of a double signpost, pointing forward and backward. In similar fashion, the horse's hoof ("fer") wounds the ground just as the poet's "faire" or "making" marks the page, while the structure of the lines is once more the reversal of a mirror image:

> *quelques bleuets, la violence*
> *de l'heure par le fer blessée*
> *tandis qu'au fond du labour s'égoutte*
> *le sang supplicié,*
> *l'heure de la mort, bleuet . . .*

> A few cornflowers, the violence
> of the hour wounded by the iron

While in the depths of the ploughing drops
the blood sacrificed,
the hour of death, cornflower . . . (D, 40)

Each text in this volume inscribes itself into a net of mirrored relationships, violent and *letteral* as well: a knife opens a "readable wound" or makes a carnal inscription as the resulting blood is splashed deliberately against a wall. As the writing surface upedged, table to wall, both surfaces reiterate the form of a page.

The odd poem called "Le Lacet" ["The Cord" or "The Shoelace"] exemplifies the intensely metatextual nature of the enterprise, *reflected upon.* It begins with a "limpid" fault or defect in a "double tale," heavily marked with cruelty. The lip uttering it is described variously as narrowed or glittering, like a streak of air; the tongue impaled is nevertheless said to be capable of excavating, and the paper betrays, even as it captures, the line of the narration: these doubled descriptions reveal the continual obsession with a duplicating ambivalence. What was originally paper-sharp, razor-thin, dangerously precise, that is, the writing line, loses its precision: "Trahison de la ligne qui s'épaissit" ["Treason of the line thickening," D, 71]. Subsequently the streak of air, line at its purest, is seen to burn brightly with the power of linking, in both positive and negative senses, for it joins and stifles, is as minimal and ferocious as a nail scratch, an "onglée," like a gesture preparing the pure incision of the plunging sea bird at the conclusion of the text. Creating a scission between lives as between lines, the bird serves to verify, to separate, and to render clear and definite:

quand plonge
l'oiseau de mer, le vérificateur
des marées
il plonge
dans ce qui s'écrit . . .
dans le schiste et le roncier,
la bataille, le récit, un champ frappé
de déshérence

rien qui ne nous sépare mieux

et brûle plus clair
il plonge, j'écris

when the sea bird
dives, verifier
of tides
he dives
in what is written . . .
in the schist and the bramble,
the battle, the tale, a field struck
with abandon

nothing separates us better
and burns clearer
he dives, I write
(D, 77)

The knife blade is whetted in a verbal reduction and sharply pointed downward as a writing tool: "n'étant qu'une lame d'air / dans l'air / affilée" ["being only a blade of air / in the air / whetted," D, 78]. Similarly, the cord itself, like a slicing string, will reappear later in a different guise, in "Pour une cassure de fond," recognizable by its fragility and delicacy of line, on the point of danger: "Je suivrai ce fil à condition / qu'il casse / qu'il éclaire le nom détruit" ["I shall follow this thread on condition / that it break / that it clarify the name destroyed," D, 137]. The destroyed name can also be read as the "non détruit," the "not destroyed" as the mirror image of what is destroyed. Later, there will survive one simple inscription, like the narrowest of scratches, the positive side of the preceding violence and sacrifice:

Une encoche	A notch
dans le buis	in the boxwood
seule	single
signe	sign (D, 131)

On the opposite page from a text beginning "meurtre non savoir," ("murder not knowledge"), as in a mirror, we read of extraction as from a tomb, where the burned land and the written land are set up themselves in opposition. The strong lead word "Extraire" ("To extract") is echoed by or mirrored in the rhyme "terre . . . terre," leading to the final isolated term "written": a recession is made from the tomb toward the writing of what is to be a "great and somber text," in which the life of the letter will presumably be lost. The elimination is simple, just a sliding down the page, toward a tomb only implicit:

Meurtre mouvement	Murder movement	
dans notre sommeil il suffit	in our sleep it is enough	
qu'un simple	for a simple	
fût d'herbe	stem of grass	
glisse	to slide	(D, 122)

This little murder can be seen to reflect the more dramatic extraction from the tomb that writing is and then to lead directly to parallel meditation on mirror, book, and tomb, another such cadence, like a *vanitas* or *memento more*:

Poncer la pierre nue de ma tombe	To pumice my tomb's bare stone	
jusqu'à ouvrir ton miroir	until your mirror opens	
tout le livre qui se referme	each book that closes	
tombe	falls	
dans le gouffre . . .	in the chasm . . .	(D, 129)

The first "tombe" or "tomb" leads to the second tomb implicit in the verb "to fall" by way of the open mirror, so that the open leads to the hidden. The cadence resounds, tenebral like a blackened glass of sound and sight, "tombe . . . tombe." Echoing within the walls of this tomb are the facing images of "terre . . . terre," the earth of burial that can be re-read now as an indication of silence, phonetically similar "taire . . . taire." The formal manner in which the transformation from homonym to homonym in all these texts is brought about relates to the nature of the envisioned reversal in the glass, for mirror and tomb, earth and silence figure each other and echo together.

The central work, "Trait pour trait" ["Stroke for Stroke"], is again a doubling of terms; it seems to respond to the text "Moraines" in *L'Embrasure.* The meditation is typographically arresting, its highly charged vocabulary intensifying the texts surrounding it. Dupin describes the artist's trace, such as that of Miró, in a way that seems appropriate to his own art, since the graphic language "is not that of the stroke choosing its support, but that of the space of the sheet relying on the stroke to reveal itself," (PS, 142). Signs, as Miró and Dupin understand them, must retain their vitality when tested upon the sheet, as in a "guerrilla warfare," which they wage against emptiness. In "Trait pour trait," the strokes or traces of the title are clarified in their relation to the art of writing:

L'exception qu'ici
en ce non-lieu m'aime
—ou le lieu d'une dérive
d'un désastre méticuleux

The exception that here
in this non-place loves me
—or the place of a deflection
of a meticulous disaster (D, 81)

These opening lines recall Mallarmé's "rien n'aura eu lieu que le lieu" ["nothing will have taken place but the place"] and his "désastre obscur" ["obscure disaster"]. A narrow cutting edge is directed against the self, itself deflected, for the "ici / m'aime" can also be read as it sounds: "ici même" or "even here." The scene is double even here. The exterior brightness ("notre grande clarté du dehors") is discerned at last through the clusters and knots of language, occupying the final position on the page, as does the light in the preceding poem, and the multiple-sensed word "relation" in the following and major poem. These three key words—light, clarity, and relation—are separated from the body of the three poems and connect to each other. Just as the exterior clarity is set in balance against the interior obscurity, so at the center of the central text of "Trait pour trait" (literally, "Stroke for Stroke," but also suggesting the line portrait [por-trait]), and itself roughly the central text of *Dehors,* the reader watches at last the picture of the "cygne" or swan emerging from the "signe" or sign or stroke. The swan sets in textual and typographic play "les fils enchevêtrés de sa fuyante / relation" ["the entangled threads of its fleeting / relation," D, 85] before reverting to a more black sign against the white margin of the page, like a wing slicing the net of relations or some "trait de scie . . ." ["stroke of the saw"].

In the other major text of *Dehors*, the writer bends over his notebooks, from the earliest to the most recent; feverishly annotating, he writes and destroys, mirrors and undoes, asking the question about his own endeavor: "a tale?" This narrator, who might be seen to repeat the gesture of the swan's wing, as "outside," is made to refer back to the writing endeavor:

> *et le cri des*
> *corneilles alentour imitant le chant éraillé*
> *plume sur de lourds feuillets de schiste . . .*

> and the cry of
> crows around imitating the scratchy sound of a
> quill pen on heavy sheets of schist . . . (D, 98)

Again the question is raised: what are we reading and writing? Is this in fact a tale or a "real description" of the making of a text? The question, "un récit?," will have only an oblique answer, and an unknown book appears, untouched and troubling. Unreadable, intense, attractive to the poet on whose imagination it preys: "un livre prédateur, dont la proximité me hante et me repousse, en entretenant une exaltation trouble, dévastatrice . . ." ["a predatory book, whose proximity haunts and repulses me, maintaining an unquiet and destructive exaltation . . . ," D, 100]. Between the white sheets of a bed, suggested by the pages of the book, a semi-erotic violence commits the reader to the reading: ("suffer . . ."). Poisonous dust and clotted blood invade the margins of the book, its empty spots and its burned slopes, mocking its mask and makeup. Whereas the former contrast of colors set white against black, here traces of red and black, like characters of a Greek vase, dance the gigue while a hanged man swings pulling the reader into the oscillation, inflicting the rhythm of the deadly dance upon his consciousness. Repeatedly the reader is sent away and the narrator is expelled from the text after his sacrifice, as his deception is marked in successive fragments:

il me chasse

. . .

l'aveugle-aveuglante paroi se fend

. . .

miroir-abîme d'une narration déjouée, miroir du simulacre

it chases me

. . .

the blind and blinding wall cracks

. . .

mirror-abyss of a narration undone, mirror of the simulacrum

(D, 101–2)

The poet continues fathering and slaughtering his text, only perhaps some mirror of a simulacrum, about always to be undone.

Whether the ritual uses table, wall, or page as its scene, no matter what authenticity it guarantees as support, the end of the scribe's original sacrifice may be only a reflection seen in a mirror, like a glass darkly and endlessly included:

> *Ce serait ta fin, ce récit, ce soupçon*
>
> . . .
>
> *Il n'y a pas de fin, tout peut reprendre, s'écrire,*
> *s'enchaîner: le cri, le calme, le dehors . . .*
>
> This would be your end, this tale, this suspicion
>
> . . .
>
> There is no end, all can start again, write
> and link itself: cry, calm, outside . . . (D, 112)

In this last work, the title is taken up like that link renewed, sending the reader back to the initial statement on which Dupin's book opens: "C'est la peau du dehors qui se retourne et nous absorbe" ["It's the skin of the outside which turns back and absorbs us"]. This organic metaphor of reading is all-enveloping, absorbing both passage as text and the concept of passage itself.

The final poem, "Malévitch," resumes all the preceding ones; beginning with death and violence, it includes the textual sacrifice, a slash upon a page, here pictured:

> *Fatal / comme en un glissement pur violent*
> *premier visage diagone* [*sic*]
>
> Fatal / like a pure violent slippage /
> first diagonal face (D, 149)

This text, with its visually enforced dispersion of images and its concern for a bare writing, becomes a window upon a still violent spectacle: "un exercice donne à traverser la faille / d'une trépanation" ["an exercise gives the gap of a trepanning / to be traversed," D, 152]. The cruel intervention of the knife as swan wing or as pen is felt even here. To that, the "laughter" or *rictus* of the violence of Malevitch's black or white crosses slashing diagonally across the page makes an answer, by a wild meditation on death. The colors are those of metaphysical poetry, and those of the artist: red, white, and black indicated and already used in this volume. Blood splashes against absence and purity, somber white makes a sign against brilliant red and deepest black. The sign itself is metaphysical; the swan's wing, white or black, represented by the black cross or incising pen, cutting or slashing across the white page, makes a narrow streak of suffering.

"Ainsi je suis dehors" ["Thus am I outside," D, 152]: at the conclusion, the long struggle toward the outer realm is complete, for poet and reader. The abyss inside and out initiates future struggles, as far as the eye and the mind can reach, ceaselessly mirroring slash and scission, duplicity and violence in the narrowest of incisions, like the line, the stroke, the scratch—in short, the sign:

> *le gouffre*
>
> . . .

le conflit encore
qui se projette blanc et noir / ou inversement blanc sur

the abyss

. . .

the conflict again
projecting itself white and black / or inversely white on

As this incomplete expression remains open on the page, the text concludes by a turn, inwardly perfected, stretching outward, like "a single sign," in an endless passage, *Dehors*.

EPILOGUE
Reading in the Passage

au long regard sans clôture
to the long look with no end
JACQUES DUPIN, *L'Embrasure*

The preceding essays on poets and on poetry retain a modest outlook, that of illustrating one metaphor of literary sensitivity among others, trying out its interconnections and extensions: from an assimilation to the rites of anthropological passage to the rituals of theatrically serious play, with its own scenic and psychological wings, the "passages" resembling the glassed-in arcades of the city and of the mind. The vast metaphor of passage provides for the exploration of landscapes outer as well as inner, through a forest, along a river, or up a mountain or across a sky, as in Char, Garelli, Deguy, and Dupin, or then, as in the work of the surrealists, along the corridors of a "Passage de l'Opéra," glimpsed as the passage of the spontaneous work. There as elsewhere, the elements flow into one another in a liquid exchange, as in the illustrations of Breton, Eluard, and Paz, and in the connecting sensitivities, as with Crane and Valéry, with Desnos and Scève, Góngora, and Apollinaire. Text links with text and perception with perception in the cobuilding of an architextural construction. For the passage serves as articulation and dwelling for the metapoetic references, to self and surround, such self-reflections needing no other mirror.

Seen by itself as an independent structure, yet in context with other like constructions, in self-support and conscious reflection, the text now read and passed along demands as constant an awareness of its architectural form as of its architextural surface, of its joins as of its grain. The observer with a predetermined view would lose the advantage of the flexible awareness responsible for the mutually interactive *building* of substance, link, and perception. Such contextural and metapoetic work as these poems seem to suggest in their mutual reworking rejects all the metaphors of structural stasis for a continuous building on and within the passage, as it is read.

NOTES

Preface

1. James Merrill's recent book *Mirabell* (New York: Atheneum, 1979) celebrates the convergence of voices and spirits communicating via the ouija board with those living, passing between present and past, life and death, individual and collective: Merrill is at least a partial inheritor, ironic but not inappropriate, of the surrealist flux.

2. I undertake an initial discussion of the threshold in this sort of text in *The Eye in the Text: Essays on Perception, Mannerist to Modern* (Princeton: Princeton University Press, 1981).

3. In Gérard Genette's recent book *Introduction à l'architexte* (Paris: Seuil, 1979), he defines the architext as the "set of general or transcendent categories to which each singular text belongs." This usage obviously appeals to the image of architecture as a stable set of ideas and theories to which individual practice conforms; as Genette rightly points out, he gives to the term a quite different sense from mine, his usage concerning only the set of poetic theories as they build on one another. I take the term in a more "textural" sense, defined at some length in the prefatory material to my *Eye in the Text*; entitled "A Poetics of Perception" (see in particular, pages 9–15). Of the first studies I published on this topic, "Vers une architexture du poème surréaliste," in *Ethique et esthétique de la littérature française du XXe siècle*, ed. Maurice Cagnon (Stanford: Anma Libri, 1977), pp. 59–68, and "Passage du poème: interrogation du seuil," *Cahiers de l'Association Internationale des Etudes Françaises*, no. 30 (May 1978): 225–243, Genette refers only to the latter, stating that he does not grasp my meaning. I hope to have made it clearer here.

4. See also Johann Freidrich Geist, *Passagen: Ein Bautyp aus 19 jahrhunderts* (Munich: Prestel, 1969). My thanks to Klaus Berger for this reference.

The Breach of the Poem

1. Gaetan Picon, *Admirable tremblement du temps*, (Paris: Skira, 1970), p. 54.

2. Jacques Garelli, *Brèche*, (Paris: Mercure de France, 1966), p. 63.

3. André Breton, *Poèmes*, (Paris: Gallimard, 1948), p. 150. Hereafter referred to as P.

4. André Breton, *Premier Manifeste*, in *Manifestes du surréalisme* (Paris: Pauvert, 1962), p. 20.

5. André Breton, *Nadja*, (Paris: Gallimard, Coll. Livre de poche, 1964), p. 155.

6. Ibid., p. 157.

7. Jacques Garelli, *La Gravitation poétique*, (Paris: Mercure de France, 1966), p. 153. Hereafter referred to as GP.

8. Yves Bonnefoy, "Les Tombeaux de Ravenne," *L'Improbable*, (Paris: Mercure de France, 1959), p. 28. It should not be necessary to trace here the relationship between the following remarks and Maurice Blanchot's general observation, akin to Jean-Paul Sartre's, that the image is the absence of what it offers us, the latter attainable only as "la présence d'une absence," or with Julia Kristeva's "Poésie et négativité" or the more tenuous link with Jean Cohen's notion of *écart* or deviation; since these have all become, like the images of the holes in the body of being, the ancestral givens of subsequent inquiry.

9. P, 104.

10. Francis Ponge, *Le Grand Recueil*, 3 (Paris: Gallimard, 1961).

11. Yves Bonnefoy, "L'Acte et le lieu de la poésie," *L'Improbable*, p. 183.

12. Yves Bonnefoy, *Du Mouvement et de l'immobilité de Douve* (Paris: *Poésie*/ Gallimard, 1970), p. 62. And on p. 68: "What is there to be desired, except that which dies, speaks, and is rent apart?"

13. See Michael Riffaterre, *Semiotics of Poetry* (Bloomington: Indiana University Press, 1978) and *La Production du texte littéraire* (Paris: Seuil, 1979).

14. Jacques Dupin, *L'Embrasure* (Paris: *Poésie*/ Gallimard, 1969), p. 64.

15. Jacques Garelli, *Les Dépossessions* (Paris: Mercure de France, 1968), p. 54. This separation once provoked, the poem plays the same role as that of the mask in Jean Starobinski's analysis of Stendhal, offering a deliberate detour, an imaginary and ephemeral deplacement of the self into a time other than the time normally lived, a space different and permitting deferment. Jeanine Jallat uses Starobinski as the basis for her remarks:

> The masked meaning is a meaning diverted, "oblique," which maintains the distance and the play between its two poles. The man of the mask "unjoins" himself to "rejoin himself," turns "himself aside" in order to "return" . . . . The space of difference has become the time of the "different" . . . the empty space of the game becomes the place of the only "fullness" because the detour is traversed by time: In the *interval*, the mask will have enabled an unfair competition with time. It will have introduced into life a gust of *discontinuity*, will have permitted . . . an imaginary time. ["Le Masque ou l'art du déplacement," *Poétique* 8 (1971):484.]

16. Jacques Derrida, *La Dissémination* (Paris: Seuil, 1972), p. 328.

17. Michel Deguy, "La Poésie en question," *Modern Language Notes*, 85, 4, (May 1970):432. Compare Jacques Derrida on the idea of the threshold, the limit, the line, and the step, in his "Pas," *Gramma* (April 1976):161–62:

> But can one, should one, *must one* land on this other shore? Would it not instantly cease being the other one? Would the event happen again? Would it not be forbidden by its arrival itself, according to the double step of the law, its double bond, its double circular knot with no circle not crossed first ("the circle of the law is this one: there must be a crossing for there to be a limit, but only the limit, insofar as it is uncrossable, summons the crossing, affirms the desire [the *faux pas*] which has already crossed the line through the unforseeable")?

The form of this commentary, typical of Derrida, is unmistakably similar to the hesitations and nuances and windings of the poetry discussed in the final pages of this volume.

18. Roland Barthes, *Le Plaisir du texte* (Paris: Seuil, 1973), passim. For example: "Isn't the most erotic place of a body found just where the clothing gapes? In perversion (which is the regime of textual pleasure) there are no 'erogenous zones' . . . intermittence is erotic, as psychoanalysis says: the skin gleaming between two pieces of clothing (the pants and the tee-shirt), between two edges (the half-opened shirt, the glove and the sleeve) . . . ," (p. 19).

From Break to Passage

1. Yves Bonnefoy, "La Fonction du poème," *Le Nuage rouge* (Paris: Mercure de France, 1977).

2. The notion of rupture has become a cliché in contemporary poetics. See the issue devoted to it by *Change* 7 (1970), the work of the Tel Quel critics, George Bataille's studies of the moment where literature reveals its limits ("défaille"), Roland Barthes's study of the gap in the garment of the text in *Le Plaisir du texte* (Paris: Seuil, 1973), and others.

3. See Rosalind Krauss, *Passages* (New York: Viking, 1977).

4. For a definition of the *relais*, this from the article on tapestry of the *Encyclopaedia Britannica* (15th ed. Macropaedia, vol. 17, p. 1056):

> Where the weft margin of a colour area is straight and parallel to the warps, it forms a kind of slit, or *relais*, which may be treated in any of five different ways. First, it may simply be left open. . . . Second, it may be left open on the loom but sewed up afterward. . . . Third, the weaver may dovetail his wefts, passing from one side and from the other in turn over a common warp. . . . The fourth treatment is interlocking or juxtaposing colour segments looped through each other and the fifth, making a solid fabric weft.

5. Compare Jacques Derrida, in "Pas," *Gramma* (April, 1976): 153–54, "There are always two steps. One in the other but without any possible inclusion, one affecting the other immediately but ready to cross it by taking its distance" with the play on steps in André Breton, *Les Pas perdus* (Paris: Gallimard, 1923).

6. In Louis Aragon, *Le Paysan de Paris* (Paris: Gallimard, 1926). Hereafter referred to as PP.

7. Henri Michaux, *Passages* (Paris: Gallimard, 1950), pp. 35–39.

8. See Arnold Van Gennep, *Les Rites du passage* (Paris: Nourry, 1909).

9. *Performance in Postmodern Culture*, ed. Michel Benamou (Milwaukee & Madison: Center for Twentieth-Century Studies and Coda Press, 1977). Here Turner refers to the work of Mihaly Csikszentmihalyi, *Beyond Boredom and Anxiety* (San Francisco: Jossey-Bass, 1975).

10. For the work of Victor Turner on "passages, margins, and poetry," see in particular: *Drama, Fields, and Metaphors* (Ithaca, N.Y.: Cornell University Press, 1974). The application of direct and indirect criteria, the sympathetic and the contagionist methods, in relation to the theory of

metonymy and metaphor remains to be worked out, but this work makes a good introduction to it. (The direct is nearer to prose, the indirect to poetry: see also Roman Jakobson's indications: "Two Aspects of Language and a Few Types of Aphasic Disturbance," in Roman Jakobson, *Fundamentals of Language* (The Hague: Mouton, 1956), pp. 55–82.)

Angus Fletcher has worked on the concept of the threshold in Edmund Spenser (*The Prophetic Moment: An Essay on Spenser* (Chicago: University of Chicago Press, 1971)), and Piero Pucci's study of the threshold in Propertius (*Glyph* 3, a journal published at Johns Hopkins University) extends the lines of the argument to classical literature.

11. I have commented at length on the importance and implications of the threshold perception in *The Eye in the Text: Essays on Perception, Mannerist to Modern* (Princeton: Princeton University Press, 1981).

Introductory Passage

1. Hart Crane, "Passage," from "White Buildings" in *The Complete Poems and Selected Letters and Prose of Hart Crane*, ed. Brom Weber (New York: Doubleday, 1966), pp. 21–22.

2. In *The Letters of Hart Crane*, ed. Brom Weber (Berkeley & Los Angeles: University of California Press, 1952), p. 215. R. W. Butterfield in *The Broken Arc: A Study of Hart Crane* (Edinburgh: Oliver & Boyd, 1969) says of Crane that in this poem "he began and failed to complete a journey in search, not of the heights of the spirit's potential, but of the deep recesses of memory and the past." Citing the widely differing attitudes of the critics, he concludes: "The poem has apparently failed to communicate even an appropriate state of mind" (p. 107). R. W. B. Lewis, *The Poetry of Hart Crane: A Critical Study* (Princeton: Princeton University Press, 1967) points out that Marianne Moore rejected this manuscript, which Crane submitted to *The Dial*, with this reasoning: "Its multiform content accounts, I suppose, for what seems to us a lack of simplicity and cumulative force," and Allen Tate cites its lack of controlling organization (Lewis, p. 187). Lewis comments at some length about the poem as a ritual and a rite, citing its "ceremonial action . . . in its rhythm of game, loss, and potential recovery" (p. 291).

I will not be so impudent as to assume that this second reading will change any reader's opinion of Crane's poem; but the comparison is enlivened by the very contrast it brings into play, between those other readings and the double image.

3. It is a commonplace that Arthur Rimbaud's influence weighed heavy upon Crane: for instance, the "Bateau ivre" upon "Voyages." See William Van O'Connor, in *Sense and Sensibility in Modern Poetry* (Chicago: University of Chicago Press, 1948), p. 73, referred to by Robert A. Day in "Image and Idea in 'Voyages II'," *Criticism* 7, 3 (Summer 1965), 225.

4. This interpretation differs from that of R. W. B. Lewis, who considers Crane's text to be centered on *hearing*.

5. Yves Bonnefoy, *Pierre écrite* (Paris: Mercure de France, 1965).

6. My thanks to John Hollander for this suggestion.

7. This sort of play is frequently found in the works of poets of the early part of the twentieth century: Reverdy, Desnos, and others.

8. Translation adapted from that by David Paul, in *Paul Valéry: An Anthology*, ed. James Lawler (Princeton: Princeton University Press, 1977).

The Poetics of a Surrealist Passage

1. André Breton, *Le Surréalisme et la peinture* (Paris: Gallimard, 1962), p. 70. Hereafter referred to as SP.

2. From "Fata Morgana," in P, 185–86.

3. André Breton, *L'Amour fou* (Paris: Gallimard, 1937), p. 85. Hereafter referred to as AF.

4. André Breton, *Perspective cavalière*, ed. Marguerite Bonnet (Paris: Gallimard, 1970).

5. Paul Eluard, *Poèmes* (Paris: Gallimard, 1951), p. 331. Hereafter referred to as E.

6. André Breton, *Les Vases communicants* (Paris: Gallimard, 1955), p. 150.

7. Louis Aragon, *Anicet ou le panorama, roman* (Paris: Gallimard, 1923), p. 22. Hereafter referred to as A.

8. Louis Aragon, *Je n'ai jamais appris à écrire, ou les incipit* (Geneva: Skira, 1969).

"One in the Other"

1. (P, 79.) Among the definitions of the passage, one of the most delicately phrased, and picturesque, is the following: ". . . et je veux bien être pendu si ce passage est autre chose qu'une méthode pour m'affranchir de certaines contraintes, un moyen d'accéder au-delà de mes forces à un domaine encore interdit. Qu'il prenne enfin son véritable nom . . .

PASSAGE
DE
L'OPÉRA ONIRIQUE

See also Peter Nesselroth, "Form and Meaning in *Le Paysan de Paris*," *Dada/Surrealism* 5 (1975):20–27, and Richard Scaldini, "'A quoi pensez-vous?' Reflections on Reading [in] Aragon's Early Prose," *Dada/Surrealism* 7 (1977):29–44. And for the formal passage, strung out, so to speak, see Michael Riffaterre's masterly "Métaphore filée dans la poésie surréaliste," *Langue française* 3 (1969):46–60, and "Anamorphoses," in *Discourse Analysis*, ed. P. R. Leon and H. Mitterand (Montréal: Centre éducatif et culturel, 1976).

For anamorphosis, see the description in, for instance, Fred Leeman, *Hidden Images, Games of Perception, Anamorphic Art, Illusion from the Renaissance to the Present* (New York: Abrams, 1976), pp. 21–22. Jeanine Plottel's studies of Raymond Roussel are particularly interesting as examples of the two techniques: see *Le Siècle éclaté* no. 1, *Le Manifeste et le caché* and no. 2 *Théorie / Tableau / Texte* (Paris: Lettres modernes, 1974 and 1978).

2. The relations between the theories and texts of Bachelard and surrealism are studied in my *Surrealism and the Literary Imagination: Gaston Bachelard and André Breton* (The Hague: Mouton, 1966). See in particular Bachelard's *L'Eau et les rêves* (Paris: Corti, 1942).

3. For some parallel illustrations of alchemy and literature, see my "In Search of the Crystal," in *Voices of Conscience*, ed. Raymond Cormier (Philadelphia: Temple University Press, 1976), pp. 241–261.

4. Denis Diderot's *Bijoux indiscrets* conducts what might be called a nonsacred conversation (as opposed to the traditional "sacra conversazione") between a magic ring and certain private jewels of the female sex: the whole thing plays on the ring in its *turn*.

5. In "Le Pitre châtié" ["The Chastised Clown"], Stéphane Mallarmé, *Oeuvres complètes* (Paris: Ed. Pléiade, 1945), p. 31.

6. See Gerard Genette on "La Reversibilité de l'image baroque" or "L'Or tombe sous le fer," in *Figures* 1 (Paris: Seuil, 1966).

7. Michael Riffaterre pointed out to me the link with La Fontaine's "soeurs lavandières," from "Le Vieux chat et la jeune souris"; quoth the cat: "Selon ces lois, descends là-bas / Meurs, et va t'en, tout de ce pas, / Haranguer les Soeurs filandières."

8. In Tristan Tzara's *Dada Manifestoes*, and in his "Note on Art" and his "Note on Poetry," the former appearing in *Dada*, no. 1 (July, 1917), the second in no. 4–5 (May, 1919), both translated in my *Approximate Man and Other Writings of Tristan Tzara* (Detroit: Wayne State, 1973), pp. 135 and 167 respectively.

9. A first reading of this poem appears in my *Surrealist Voice of Robert Desnos* (Amherst: University of Massachusetts Press, 1977), pp. 96–100. This is a reinterpretation, but the readings may also be taken *one in the other*.

Rites of a Flowing Element

1. The flowers here are the exact opposite of Charles Baudelaire's romantic-symbolist "Fleurs du mal," being the flowers "de la mer," thus of the feminine as opposed to the masculine, and even of a rebirth into the maternal world, as *mère* is traditionally implied in the word *mer*, so the presence of the one in the other here is inescapable.

2. Compare the ending of Desnos's poem "Jamais d'autre que toi" in *Domaine public* (Paris: Gallimard, 1943), p. 147. Hereafter cited as DP.

> *Jamais jamais d'autre que toi*
> *Et moi seul seul seul comme le lierre fané des jardins de banlieue*
> *seul comme le verre*
> *Et toi jamais d'autre que toi.*

The final desolation is ironically prepared by an initial vow of fidelity, "never anyone but you," then transposed to the lamentation of the self alone. See, in this volume, the comparison of Desnos and of Góngora, poet of *Las Soledades*.

3. The exceptional length and weight of these lines are reminiscent of the even longer-flowing line of "Je t'apporte . . ." in "Idée fixe," where the algae from the sea's depths are brought to the lady seated before the mirror. The build-up of these exceptional sentences is quite unlike that of the sevenfold accumulations in the construction of Desnos's response to Remy de Gourmont's "Litanie de la rose" in the repeated roses of "De la rose de marbre à la rose de fer" or the one-by-one additions of elements to the celebration of "Isabelle la vague" in the highly patterned "Avec un coeur de chêne." Both these accretions are worked out during the entire length of the poem's pattern, whereas the exceptional length and weight of the line here accentuate a single moment of the poem as the emotional and formal center for the surrounding flux, a center haunting in its fixity. See my study of Desnos's structures in my *Surrealist Voice of Robert Desnos* (Amherst: University of Massachusetts, 1977).

4. About the potential myth of the bottle, as it contains by implication both mermaid and message, both intoxication and poetry itself, see the book listed in the preceding note.

5. The Muriel Rukeyser version gives, in translation for this line, the following: "Like the April surf. . . ." It is regrettable that the echo of "marejada . . . marzo" is lost in English. A passage of Ovid echoes here.

6. As for the cosmic relations of jade itself both to the universe and to man in ancient Chinese philosophy, the solar properties are supposed to link it to the transcendent, the sun lasting through the night of Paz's poem and the night of jade here; the images here tend toward a baroque illumination, as if the dazzling darkness were to be metamorphosed by a profoundly green water, by sun, and by stone and by the plant of jade.

7. In a letter of January, 1981, James Merrill reminds me of the nine openings in the body, as they were thought of in ancient times; my warm thanks to him for the reminder. Washing lye (mordent) has its own bite.

8. As the "marejada" turns finally to the "jade" in the profound darkness, and as Breton's implicit "mâle" leads to his explicit "malle" and "mal" in his text analyzed in these pages, so the "green/leaf" implicit in the Merrill poem passes over and into the "lean/grief," which carries all the force of the poem in its concluding and yet central passage.

9. As an example, finally, of encounter, and mutual illumination, the essay of Octavio Paz on Breton: "André Breton or the Quest of the Beginning," in *Alternating Current*, trans. Helen Lane (New York: Grove/Viking, 1973) is one of the most ardent testimonies both to Breton himself ("It is impossible to write about André Breton in any other language than that of passion," 47), Breton as a Mannerist poet (p. 51), as a poet of *revelation*, and as a poet of the "*other* time," and to the enduring of surrealism itself. ". . . to me Surrealism was the sacred malady of our world, like leprosy in the Middle Ages or the state of possession of the Spanish Illumination in the sixteenth century; since it was a necessary negation in the West, (I told

him that) it would remain alive as long as modern civilization remained alive, whatever political systems and ideologies might prevail in the future, [p. 54]."

Ode to a Surrealist Baroque

1. Louis Aragon, *Le Paysan de Paris* (Paris: Gallimard, 1926). Hereafter referred to as PP.

2. Robert Desnos, *La Liberté ou l'amour!* (Paris: Gallimard, 1928). Hereafter referred to as LA.

3. Maurice Scève, *Délie* in *Oeuvres poétiques* (Paris: Slatkine repr., 1972). Dizain CCCCXXI.

4. Robert Desnos, *Corps et biens* (Paris: *Poésie*/Gallimard, 1968), p. 51.

5. For a similar play on eyes and words, see the study of the exchange between the eyes of poet and reader in my essay called *The Eye in the Text: Essays on Perception, Mannerist to Modern* (Princeton: Princeton University Press, 1981).

6. The examples given by Louis Martz, *The Wit of Love* (Notre Dame, Ind.: Notre Dame University Press, 1962). Gesualdo furnishes a good example of the privileged technique of changeability or *cangiantismo*, of passing from one form and hue to another: the eye does not rest. Compare Mario Praz, *Mnemosyne* (Princeton: Princeton University Press, 1970). chapter 4. For an intriguing study on Scève's wandering line, see Richard Klein, "Straight Lines and Arabesques: Metaphors of Metaphor," in *Yale French Studies*, Language as Action issue 45 (1970):64–86.

7. Robert Desnos, *Reflexions sur la poésie*, in *Destinée arbitraire*, ed. M. C. Dumas (Paris: *Poésie*/Gallimard, 1977), pp. 237–38.

8. Maurice Molho quotes these lines in his "Concept et métaphore dans Góngora," *Europe*, no. Góngora (1977): 106, and uses this diagram.

9. Ibid., pp. 115–17.

10. Further similarities could be traced between Góngora and Desnos on the basis of Molho's analysis, such as, for instance, the play between silence and the word: "Le poème *dicible* est *silence*, le poème *dit* est *parole* . . . ." See my analysis of Desnos's voice and silence in *The Surrealist Voice of Robert Desnos* (Amherst: University of Massachusetts Press, 1977).

In relation to Desnos's obsession with shipwreck, and in an implicit reference back to Mallarmé, see also Pierre Darmangeat, "Divagation sur un naufrage," in the Góngora number of *Europe*. In the light of these themes, one of the strongest currents leading from symbolism to surrealism is clearly visible: the fact that the connections with the baroque are so omnipresent has been insufficiently stressed.

Apollinaire and His Readers

1. Tristan Tzara, *Oeuvres complètes*, ed. Henri Béhar (Paris: Flammarion, 1975), p. 209.

2. René Char, *La Nuit talismanique* (Geneva: Skira, 1972), p. 12.

3. Guillaume Apollinaire, *Les Peintres cubistes* (Paris: Figuière, 1913, new edition, Geneva: Cailler, 1950), p. 10. Hereafter referred to as PC.

4. Jean-Claude Chevalier, *Alcools d'Apollinaire: Essai d'analyse des formes poétiques*. (Paris: Lettres modernes, 1970).

5. See the chapter on Char's baroque imagery in my *Eye in the Text: Essays on Perception, Mannerist to Modern* (Princeton: Princeton University Press, 1981).

6. Paul Eluard, *Oeuvres complètes* I (Paris: ed. Pléiade, 1968), p. 1032. Hereafter referred to as OC.

7. Guillaume Apollinaire, *Oeuvres poétiques* (Paris: ed. Pléiade, 1965), p. 108. Hereafter referred to as OP.

8. Louis Aragon, *Mouvement perpétuel* (Paris: *Poésie*/Gallimard), p. 43.

9. "J'appelle à moi les tornades et les ouragans . . . /j'appelle à moi les amours et les amoureux/j'appelle à moi les vivants et les morts/j'appelle les fossoyeurs j'appelle les assassins . . . ," Robert Desnos, DP, 109.

10. Breton, *Nadja* (Paris: Gallimard, 1928), p. 154.

11. For a study of the destructive endings of Desnos, see my *Surrealist Voice of Robert Desnos*, (Amherst: University of Massachusetts Press, 1977).

12. LeRoy Breunig, "The Laughter of Apollinaire," *Yale French Studies*, Surrealism issue, (Spring 1964):66–73.

13. Desnos, DP, 139. Not only do the images of Apollinaire and Desnos correspond intimately, but also so do certain of their poetic structures, such as those of condensation and repetition. Compare, for example, Apollinaire's "Deuxième poème secret," "O ma chère Deïté chère et farouche intelligence de l'univers qui m'est réservé comme tu m'es réservé . . . ," with Desnos's "Douleurs de l'amour!," "O douleurs de l'amour! Comme vous m'êtes nécessaires et comme vous m'êtes chères." Or compare the same poem with its extraordinary rhapsody addressed to the woman's hair, with Desnos's "Idée fixe" and its obsession with the arrangement of the hair; the image remains also, obsessively, in the reader's mind.

René Char

1. The works referred to are the following, in order: René Char, *Aromates chasseurs* (Paris: Gallimard, 1975). Hereafter referred to as AC; René Char, *Poems of René Char*, translated and annotated by Mary Ann Caws and Johnathan Griffin (Princeton: Princeton University Press, 1976). Hereafter referred to as RC; René Char, *Recherche de la base et du sommet* (Paris: Gallimard, 1962). Hereafter referred to as RBS; Herman Melville, "White Jacket," in *Selected Tales and Poems* (New York: Rinehart, 1950).

2. The revisions to "L'Etoile de mer" are shown in a note to the poem, as further examples of the poet's passage through his own texts.

3. Peter Caws helped immeasurably in the translation of these texts, which can be found in their final form in *Chants de la Balandrane* (Paris: Gallimard, 1978), p. 65 and p. 69 respectively.

4. The entire letter, of primary importance for the understanding of Char's attitude, is translated in my book *René Char* (Boston: Twayne, 1977).

5. *Moby Dick*, in *Romances of Herman Melville* (New York: Little & Ives, 1931), p. 760.

6. The poem is commented on at some length in my book *Presence of René Char* (Princeton: Princeton University Press, 1976).

7. Typical of the self-examination in the texts themselves, Char revised this poem in the publication *Chants de la Balandrane*. The last stanza of the first version, one line shorter than the final version, begins: "Lève la tete, passant pauvre," an expression subsequently changed to read "passant de fortune," which will figure as the last few words in the final revision—for here, the "artisan moite" replaces that poor and then accidental passerby, and the last line "Cadeau d'un passant de fortune," is added after the salt-tinged star on which the original poem ended. The poet is thus finally a passerby in his own texts.

8. Char prefers the simple girl's name Madeleine, because de La Tour pictures her, he says, before her conversion. (In a private conversation.)

9. The Courbet painting is called "Les Casseurs de pierres." The artist describes it in a letter to M. and Mme Francis Wey, d'Ornans of November 26, 1849:

> *Là est un vieillard de soixante et dix ans, courbé sur son travail, la masse en l'air, les chairs hâlées par le soleil, sa tête à l'ombre d'un chapeau de paille; son pantalon de rude étoffe est tout rapiécé; puis dans ses sabots fêlés, des bas qui furent bleus laissent voir les talons. Ici, c'est un jeune homme à la tete poussiéreuse, au teint bis; la chemise dégoûtante et en lambeaux lui laisse voir les flancs et les bras; une bretelle en cuir retient les restes d'un pantalon, et les souliers de cuir boueux étirent tristement de bien des côtés. Le vieillard est à genoux, le jeune homme est derrière lui, debout, portant avec énergie un panier de pierres cassées. Hélas! dans cet état, c'est ainsi qu'on commence, c'est ainsi qu'on finit!* [Imagine an old man, about seventy or thereabouts, bent over his work with his sledge-hammer raised, his skin deeply tanned, his head shaded with a straw hat, his pants of rough cloth mended in many places; in his dilapidated clog shoes, his heels show through his faded blue stockings. Then a young man with a dusty face and tawny complexion, whose dirty ragged shirt shows his torso and arms; one leather suspender holds up what remains of a pair of pants, and his shoes of muddy leather gape sadly on all sides. The old man is kneeling, the young one standing behind him, vigorously hoisting up a basket of broken stones. Alas! if you begin like this, that is the way you end!] (*Courbet raconté par lui-même et par ses amis* [Geneva: Pierre Cailler, 1952], pp. 75–76).

Here, in closing, the last poem of *Aromates chasseurs* comes back to mind, as the open shoes of which this poet speaks recall not only those of Rimbaud, but those seen by Courbet. The artist and poets are "correspondants" and "alliés substantiels." "Tu t'établirais dans ta page, sur les bords d'un ruisseau, comme l'ambre gris sur le varech échoué; puis, la nuit montée, tu t'éloignerais des habitants insatisfaits, pour un oubli servant d'étoile. Tu n'entendrais plus geindre tes souliers entrouverts" ["You would settle in your page, on the banks of a stream, like ambergris in the stranded seaweed; then when night had risen, you would withdraw from the unsatisfied inhabitants, for an oblivion serving as a star. No longer would you hear the complaint of your gaping shoes" AC, 43].

10. My *Presence of René Char* contains a chapter called the "Cycle by the Hand," and another section entitled "Passage by the Hand." The image of the hand is of primary importance in this poetry.

11. Stéphane Mallarmé, *Igitur, Divagations . . .* (Paris: *Poésie* / Gallimard, 1976), p. 123.

12. *La Nuit talismanique* (Geneva: Skira, 1972), p. 16.

13. Rene Char, *Faire du chemin avec . . .* (Avignon: Librarie "Le Parvis," 1976). Hereafter referred to as FD. in *Fenêtres dormantes et porte sur le toit* (Paris: Gallimard, 1980), p. 11.

14. The text ends with "In Extremis la scarabée," referred to here; thus the ashes are, at their origin, close to the initial fire, completing its cycle. Thus each production is a complete path; I have taken the examination of Char's path further, through his texts of 1980, in my book *René Char: "l'oeuvre filante"* (Paris: Nizet, 1981).

15. The poetry demands it; the idea of a poetic partnership between author and reader should be advocated and defended with passion.

Jacques Garelli

1. The epigraph, by Jacques Garelli, is from *Brèche* (Paris: Mercure de France, 1966). Hereafter referred to as B. The following texts by Garelli are also cited: *La Gravitation poétique* (Paris: Mercure de France, 1970); *Les Dépossessions, suivis de Prendre appui* (Paris: Mercure de France, 1968). Hereafter referred to as LD and PA; *Lieux précaires, suivis de la Pluie belliqueuse du souviendras* (Paris: Mercure de France, 1972). Hereafter referred to as LP and LPB; *Difficile séjour* (published by *L'Action poétique*, Sept. 1977). Hereafter referred to as DS (read in manuscript).

2. To avoid the possible misinterpretations occasioned by such words as symbol, image, and metaphor, when Garelli wishes to speak of this temporal structure of consciousness, of the phonetic and semantic tension produced by the explosive manifestations of poetic time, he deliberately chooses a designation uncharged with meaning, "dépourvue de toute réalité ontique . . . le N.I.A.S.T.V. (Noyau Intentionnel à Articulations Sonores de Tensions Variables)."

Michel Deguy

1. Works referred to by Michel Deguy include: *Fragment du cadastre* (Paris: Gallimard, 1960). Hereafter referred to as FC; *Poèmes de la presqu'île* (Paris: Gallimard, 1961). Hereafter referred to as DEPP; *Actes* (Paris: Gallimard, 1961). Hereafter referred to as DEA; *Biefs* (Paris: Gallimard, 1964). Hereafter referred to as DEB; *Góngora, Revue de poésie* 60 (Sept. 1966). Hereafter referred to as DEG; *Figurations* (Paris: Gallimard, 1969). Hereafter referred to as F; *Poèmes* (Paris, Gallimard, 1972). Hereafter referred to as DEP; *Jumelages, suivis de Made in USA* (Paris: Seuil, 1978).

2. Compare also with Marcelin Pleynet, *Comme*, (Paris: Seuil, 1965).

3. Michel Deguy, "La Poésie en question," *Modern Language Notes* 85, 4, (May 1970): 432. See also *L'Enseignement de la littérature* (Paris: Plon, 1972), p. 417, for a discussion of the *lisière*.

4. "Pratique de la poésie," p. 6.

5. "Le poème du poème": the expression is that of Michel Deguy.

6. See André Breton's fascination with the "envers" and the "endroit," the recto and verso, of the piece of writing, and his question as to what passes through:

> *Qu'est-ce qui est écrit?*
>
> *Il y a ce qui est écrit sur nous et ce que nous écrivons*
> *Où est la grille qui montrerait que si son tracé extérieur*
> *Cesse d'être juxtaposable à son tracé intérieur*
> *La main passe*
>
> What is written?
>
> There is what is written on us and what we write
> Where is the grid which would show that if its outer trace
> Ceases to be juxtaposable with its inner trace
> The hand passes. (P, 125)

See "Surrealism's Outlook and Inscape," in my book *The Eye in the Text: Essays on Perception, Mannerist to Modern*, (Princeton: Princeton University Press, 1981).

7. See two essays with opposite judgments of Deguy's *Jumelages*: Yves Michaud, "Michel Deguy: "Qu'il faut toujours faire deux choses à la fois (au moins)" and Pierre Pachet, "Gaffe injure attention" in *Critique*, (June–July 1979) nos. 385–386: "30 ans de Poésie française, Des Singuliers au pluriel."

8. Yves Bonnefoy's *Arrière-Pays* (Geneva: Skira, 1973) offers a profound and subtle study of the crossroads as place of difference between the elements of here and there, continued on a different plane in his book *Dans le leurre du seuil* (Paris: Mercure de France, 1975). I have attempted to situate the importance of these works in my book *Yves Bonnefoy* (Boston: Twayne, 1982).

Jacques Dupin

1. All other poetic references will be taken from the following volumes by Jacques Dupin: *Gravir* (Paris: Gallimard, 1963). Hereafter referred to as G, *L'Embrasure, précédé de Gravir* (Paris: *Poésie* / Gallimard, 1971). Hereafter referred to as E; *L'Embrasure* (Paris: Gallimard, 1969). Hereafter referred to as EG; *L'Ephémère*, ed. Maeght, 19–20 (1972). Hereafter referred to as EP; *Dehors* (Paris: Gallimard, 1975). Hereafter referred to as D. A good study of Dupin and his significance in contemporary French poetry is to be found in Robert Greene's book *Six French Poets of Our Time* (Princeton: Princeton University Press, 1978).

2. This task corresponds topographically to René Char's *Recherche de la base et du sommet* (Paris: *Poésie* / Gallimard, 1962) and to his *Retour amont*, in *Le Nu perdu* (Paris: Gallimard, 1972) as well as to André du Bouchet's series of meditations over a number of years on the ascent of the mountain, and

to that of Jacques Garelli in his *Lieux précaires* (Paris: Mercure de France, 1972).

3. For Jacques Garelli also, the support is verbal: *Prendre appui*—the crumbling action here and the emphasis on the passage downward may remind the reader of the title of Dupin's recent play *L'Eboulement*, signifying roughly the same thing.

4. Compare Jacques Dupin's "L'Urne," the image of a poem as a passionate place for verbal sacrifice, where the urn as a mouth speaking in poetic fervor opens the passage to an inert and yet lucid consumption:

> *Mais la bouche à la fin, la bouche pleine de terre*
> *Et de fureur,*
> *Se souvient que c'est elle qui brûle*
> *Et guide les berceaux sur le fleuve.*
>
> But the mouth at last, the mouth filled with earth
> And of fury,
> Remembers that it is burning
> And guides the cradles on the river. (E, 45)

INDEX

LIBRARY OF CONGRESS CATALOGING IN PUBLICATION DATA

Caws, Mary Ann.
A metapoetics of the passage.

Includes index.
1. Poetry, Modern—History and criticism.
2. Surrealism (Literature). 3. French poetry—20th century—History and criticism. I. Title.
PN1161.C3 809.1'91 80-54468
ISBN 0-87451-194-1 AACR2

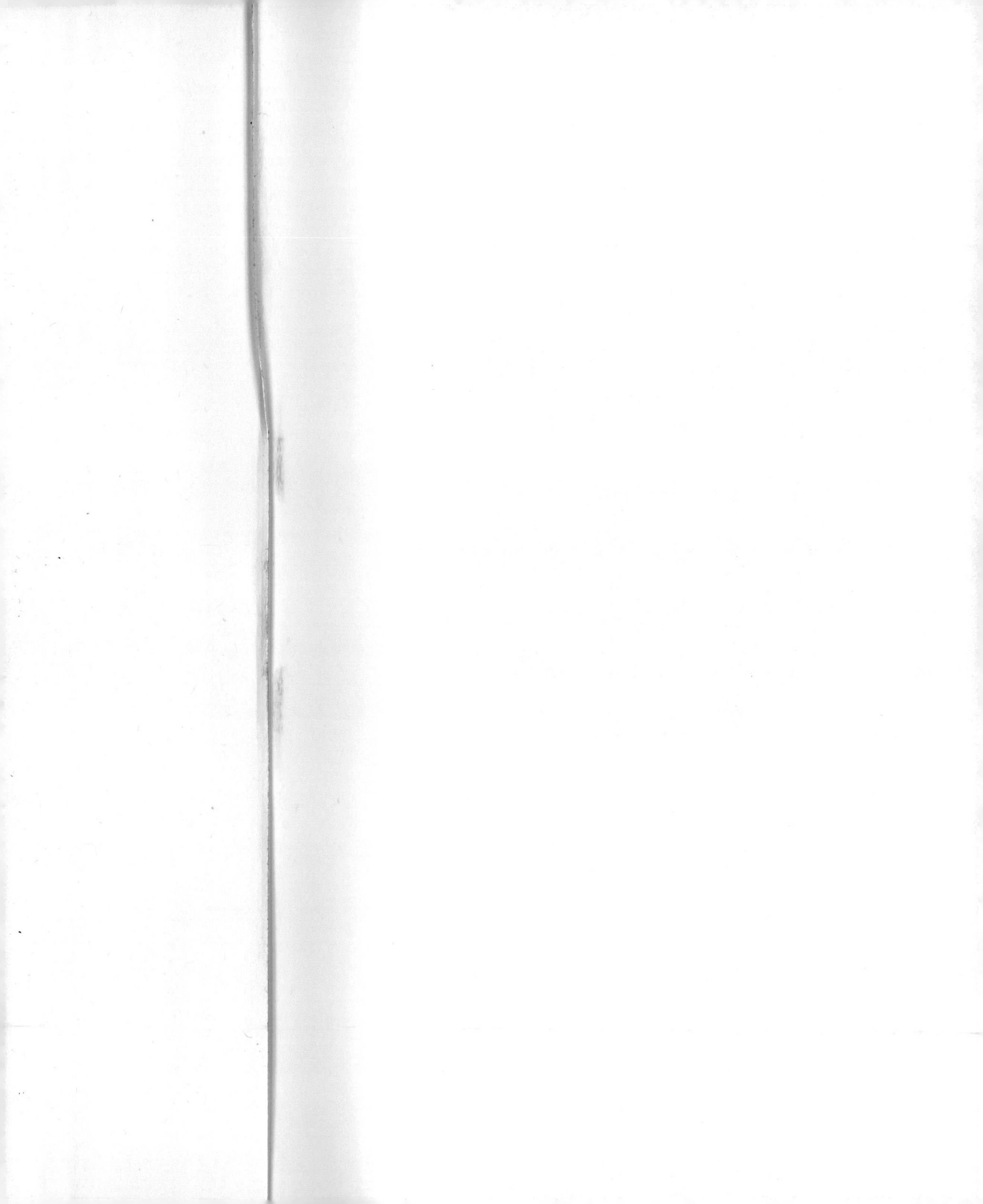